Ethnography, Superdiversity and Linguistic Landscapes

CRITICAL LANGUAGE AND LITERACY STUDIES

Series Editors: Professor Alastair Pennycook, *University of Technology, Sydney, Australia*; Professor Brian Morgan, *Glendon College/York University, Toronto, Canada* and Professor Ryuko Kubota, *University of British Columbia, Vancouver, Canada*

Critical Language and Literacy Studies is an international series that encourages monographs directly addressing issues of power (its flows, inequities, distributions, trajectories) in a variety of language- and literacy-related realms. The aim with this series is twofold: (1) to cultivate scholarship that openly engages with social, political and historical dimensions in language and literacy studies, and (2) to widen disciplinary horizons by encouraging new work on topics that have received little focus (see below for partial list of subject areas) and that use innovative theoretical frameworks.

Full details of all the books in this series and of all our other publications can be found on http://www.multilingual-matters.com, or by writing to Multilingual Matters, St Nicholas House, 31–34 High Street, Bristol BS1 2AW, UK.

Ethnography, Superdiversity and Linguistic Landscapes

Chronicles of Complexity

Jan Blommaert

MULTILINGUAL MATTERS
Bristol • Buffalo • Toronto

In memory of Jens Normann Jørgensen

Library of Congress Cataloging in Publication Data
Blommaert, Jan.
Ethnography, Superdiversity and Linguistic Landscapes: Chronicles of Complexity/Jan Blommaert.
Critical Language and Literacy Studies: 18
Includes bibliographical references and index.
1. Multilingualism–Belgium–Antwerp. 2. Languages in contact–Belgium–Antwerp. 3. City dwellers–Language–Belgium–Antwerp. 4. Linguistic minorities–Belgium–Antwerp. 5. Ethnicity–Belgium–Antwerp. 6. Sociolinguistics–Belgium–Antwerp. 7. Antwerp (Belgium)–Languages. I. Title.
P115.5.B4B56 2013
306.44'609493222–dc23 2013022862

British Library Cataloguing in Publication Data
A catalogue entry for this book is available from the British Library.

ISBN-13: 978-1-78309-040-2 (hbk)
ISBN-13: 978-1-78309-039-6 (pbk)

Multilingual Matters
UK: St Nicholas House, 31–34 High Street, Bristol BS1 2AW, UK.
USA: UTP, 2250 Military Road, Tonawanda, NY 14150, USA.
Canada: UTP, 5201 Dufferin Street, North York, Ontario M3H 5T8, Canada.

The policy of Multilingual Matters/Channel View Publications is to use papers that are natural, renewable and recyclable products, made from wood grown in sustainable forests. In the manufacturing process of our books, and to further support our policy, preference is given to printers that have FSC and PEFC Chain of Custody certification. The FSC and/or PEFC logos will appear on those books where full certification has been granted to the printer concerned.

Typeset by Techset Composition India (P) Ltd., Bangalore and Chennai, India.
Printed and bound in Great Britain by Short Run Press Ltd.

Contents

Preface and Acknowledgments

It took me a long time to write this small book, and the reasons for this will be discussed in the pages of this study. One has a tendency to assume that one's everyday habitat is a well-known place that holds few, if any, mysteries to its inhabitants. I believe I held this silly idea when I formed the plan, several years ago, of devoting a book-length study to my own neighborhood in Antwerp. I had to abandon that idea rather quickly, for my neighborhood proved to be astonishingly complex and impossible to 'describe' in a traditional sense – that is, using the synchronic descriptive stance that provides the bread and butter of sociolinguistics.

Thus, while I tried to study something very local – the streets around my house – I began to see the wider, indeed fundamental relevance of the exercise. In order to study my own space adequately, several major methodological and epistemological interventions were required. I had, for instance, to shift from a focus on mobility, articulated in several earlier works of mine, to what I now see as its logical extension: complexity. And in a way, strangely, this brought me back to some very old interests I had, in my student years, in chaos and complexity theory. It sometimes takes a decade to move from one intellectual position to another, even if the distance between these positions appears to be minimal after the fact. And then, one finds oneself in a familiar place – a new intellectual position that is in effect a very old one. It has been a sobering experience indeed.

Getting there was entirely a matter of teamwork. The work on sociolinguistic superdiversity that I have been doing over the past handful of years has, from day one, been part of the activities of what became INCOLAS – the International Symposium for Language and Superdiversity. Themes and approaches to them were discussed on a regular basis, since 2009, with that wonderful troupe of colleagues and friends who collaborate with me under the INCOLAS umbrella: Ben Rampton, Roxy Harris, Sirpa Leppänen, Adrian Blackledge, Angela Creese, Marilyn Martin-Jones, Jens Normann Jørgensen,

Martha Karrebaek, Lian Madsen, Janus Møller, Christopher Stroud, Karel Arnaut, David Parkin, Steven Vertovec and their collaborators. My own team of colleagues in Tilburg was evidently the first critical audience throughout, and the contributions of Sjaak Kroon, Max Spotti, Piia Varis, Jef Van der Aa, Fie Velghe, Xuan Wang, Caixia Du, Kasper Juffermans, Dong Jie, Jinling Li, Jos Swanenberg, Paul Post and April Huang have been crucial. People who are close in our field but less close to home were also important providers of feedback throughout the process: Alastair Pennycook, Adam Jaworski, Nik Coupland, Gunther Kress, Michael Silverstein, Asif Agha, Lionel Wee, Rob Moore, Ron Scollon, Pan Lin, Stephen May and Monica Barni all fed me with ideas and insights that left traces in this book. And Frederik, Alexander and Pika, along with several neighbors from Berchem, were continuously sharp and critical listeners and readers of what I had to say about our neighborhood.

Some parts of this book have been previously published. An earlier version of Chapter 2 was published as Blommaert and Huang (2010), 'Historical bodies and historical space', *Journal of Applied Linguistics* 6 (3), 11–26. Important parts of Chapter 3 appeared as Blommaert and Huang (2010), 'Semiotic and spatial scope: towards a materialist semiotics', *Working Papers in Urban Language and Literacies* 62. A version of Chapter 5 appeared as 'Infrastructures of superdiversity: Conviviality and language in an Antwerp neighborhood', *European Journal of Cultural Studies* (2013). An abridged version of Chapter 6, finally, appeared as Blommaert (2011), The Vatican of the diaspora. *Jaarboek voor Liturgieonderzoek* 27, 243–259. I am deeply indebted to April Huang for allowing me to republish the co-authored papers in this single-authored book, as well as to Equinox Publishers, SAGE, and to the Instituut voor Christelijk Cultureel Erfgoed, Groningen and the Instituut voor Liturgische en Rituele Studies, Tilburg, for permission to use these published papers here.

A final word of thanks is due to my series editors Alastair Pennycook, Brian Morgan and Ryuko Kubota, and to Tommi Grover, Anna Roderick and Sarah Williams of Multilingual Matters for accepting this small book in what I consider to be the most outstanding book series on language and globalization, and for seeing me through the editing and production process. I am very proud to join the ranks of authors in the exquisite Critical Language and Literacy Studies series.

If readers find this a book worth reading, it is owing to the people I have mentioned here; if not, I am happy to take the blame myself and accept that it is a poor book in spite of the massive input and support of this large team. It is for the reader to judge now.

Jan Blommaert
Berchem, March 2013

Series Editors' Preface

Linguistic landscape research has taken off in the last few years. There seem to be several reasons for this: first, an increased attention to space, location and the physical environment. Some 10 years ago, Scollon and Scollon called for 'progressively more acute analyses of the ways in which places in time and space come to have subjective meanings for the humans who live and act within them' (Scollon & Scollon, 2003: 12). This was a move aimed to understand in much greater depth the role of space and place in relation to language. Where previously a lot of sociolinguistic work had tended to operate with a rather underexamined notion of 'context', this new orientation urged us to explore the relation between signs and their place in space much more carefully. Second, a growing interest in urban multilingualism, coupled with a focus on linguistic ethnography, increased our awareness of the need to explore the lived experience of languages in the city rather than the demolinguistic mapping of variety. Third, a focus on language policy in relation to public signs started to draw attention to the ways in which different languages were represented in public spaces. The problem of English or other dominant languages also became a focus here, with attention turning to the ways in which advertising, for example, often thrust English into the public domain at the expense of other languages.

The notion of linguistic landscapes has clearly resonated with researchers interested in social and political roles of languages (Shohamy & Gorter, 2009): it emphasizes that language is not something that exists only in people's heads, in texts written for institutional consumption or in spoken interactions, but rather is part of the physical environment. At least in urban contexts – as Coulmas (2009) points out, a better term might indeed be *linguistic cityscape* – language surrounds us, directs us, hales us, calls for our attention, flashes its messages to us. Linguistic landscapes take us into the spatiality of language; we are invited to explore what Scollon and Scollon (2003: 12) called *geosemiotics*: 'an integrative view of these multiple semiotic systems which together form the meanings which we call place'. As Shohamy and Gorter (2009: 4) explain, linguistic landscape (LL) 'contextualizes the public space within issues of identity and language policy of nations, political and social conflicts ... LL is a broader concept than documentation of signs; it incorporates multimodal theories to include sounds, images, and graffiti'.

From these beginnings, attention to the LL has now become not only a focus in itself but also part of a broader sociolinguistic toolkit to study anything from graffiti (Jørgensen[1], 2008; Pennycook, 2010) to Welsh teahouses in Patagonia (Coupland, 2013), the semiotic landscape of airports (Jaworski & Thurlow, 2013) or the Corsican tourist scene (Jaffe & Oliva, 2013). Despite this productive space that the idea of LLs has opened up, there are nonetheless some more critical questions that need to be asked. One basic concern – and another reason that has led to the growth of LL research – is the ease of using digital cameras as research tools (no need for interviews, ethnographies, field notes, transcriptions, translations: just press a button, download, insert, and it's done). Linguistic landscape research, therefore, has perhaps at times been too easy. In this context, however, the benefits of LL research as an accessible pedagogical strategy should also be appreciated. Elana Shohamy's accounts (many personal communications) of her students heading out across Tel Aviv and other towns, cities and villages with their cameras and smart phones, give strong testimony to its usefulness as the students return with stories, images, new awarenesses and politicizations of the LLs of Israel.

At the same time, the ways in which the study of LLs has often proceeded has constrained the possibilities of seeing LLs in more dynamic terms. Both the concept of language embedded in the 'linguistic' and the concept of context embedded in the 'landscape' have been commonly viewed from perspectives that limit the possibilities of thinking about language and place in more vibrant ways. A common construction of language in this work, for example, has been as an indicator of a particular language, with the focus then being on the representation of different languages in public space as part of an attempt to address questions about which languages are used for particular public duties, how official language policies are reflected in public signs, how local sign-making may present other forms of diversity, and so on. While interesting enough questions in themselves, this sort of LL research leaves many other questions hanging: Can we so readily identify the language of a sign and assume the consequences of using one language or another (Pennycook, 2009)? Which signs are more salient and how do people read them? Who writes the signs and why? How do we interact with the LL we inhabit? Malinowski's (2009) question 'Who authors the landscape?', therefore, becomes not only a question as to who has written what sign but how our landscapes are made through language. In order to understand signs in landscapes, we need signographies (ethnographies of signs) rather than sign cartographies (maps of signs).

Which brings us to Blommaert's work. He has long argued (e.g. 2005) that in order to understand texts, signs or discourses, we cannot rely solely on textual analysis: rather we need textual ethnographies. In a significant critique of some of the textual and analytic myopias of critical discourse analysis, therefore, Blommaert has suggested that critical analysis needs to get beyond 'the old idea that a chunk of discourse has only *one* function and *one* meaning' (2005: 34), and that 'linguists have no monopoly over theories of language' (2005: 35). He goes on to suggest that there are therefore a range of candidates to provide an understanding of how language works, and that 'if we wish to understand contemporary forms of inequality in and through language,' we should look not only inside language but outside (in society) as well (2005: 35). This comment echoes the earlier remark by Bourdieu: 'As soon as one treats language as an autonomous object, accepting the radical separation which Saussure made between internal and external linguistics, between the science of language and the science of the social uses of language, one is condemned to looking within words for the power of words, that is, looking for it where it is not to be found' (1991: 107).

The need to understand signs, discourses and language ethnographically, from the outside as well as the inside, is one of the central arguments of this new book, where Blommaert brings to the domain of LL research an insistence on the need for 'deep ethnographic immersion'. There are two sides to this: on the one hand the need to grasp the situated and momentary occurrence of a sign in this shop window, on this street, at this time; on the other hand a need to situate these observations within a much longer historical trajectory, so that we can also grasp the layers of history and meaning at play in a sign, as well as its locational history and the broad array of meanings it indexes across time and space. This brings us to the second major focus of this work – in part an obvious result of (or precursor to) the ethnographic focus – the idea of complexity. Here, linking to the theme of superdiversity, Blommaert argues we need to try to account for the complexity of forces and meanings that dynamically come to bear on the instance of a sign and its interpretation, noting the simultaneous operation of multi-scaled and polycentric systems of meaning, a conceptual approach conveyed through his notions of 'ordered indexicalities' and 'layered simultaneity'.

The idea of complexity, in which non-linear, recursive and emergent forms of meaning making are foregrounded, is crucially important not only for understanding LLs, but also for how we teach and learn second/additional languages, particularly in the super-diversifying, cosmopolitan spaces that Blommaert details. Towards this goal, areas of complementarity and application can be noted: for example, in Diane Larsen-Freeman's (2012) work on complexity and chaos theory in SLA, and her dynamic and emergent notion of 'grammaring' for pedagogy; in Mark Clarke's (2003) innovative adaptation of Gregory Bateson's systems theory for language teacher education; and in the late, Leo van Lier's (2004, 2011) ground-breaking work on the ecology and semiotics of language learning and its possibilities for expanding the scope of ELT practice: 'It is clear that an ecological and semiotic stance on language learning is anchored in agency, as all of life is. Teaching, in its very essence, is promoting agency. Pedagogy is guiding this agency wisely' (2011: 391). The idea of complexity, so conceived, is not a loss of rigor but instead a source of empowerment, an epistemology by which social agents may recognize and re-imagine possibilities for change.

The Critical Language and Literacy Series is most fortunate to have *Ethnography, Superdiversity and Linguistic Landscapes* on its list. Another important aspect of this book is the intellectual trajectory of which it is a part, the complexity of polycentric systems of meaning that dynamically come to bear on this text. In a series of major works Blommaert (2005, 2008, 2010) has drawn attention to the need to understand language ethnographically, locally, historically, and in relation to mobility. As he argues, language is best understood sociolinguistically as *'mobile speech,* not as static language, and lives can consequently be better investigated on the basis of repertoires set against a real historical and spatial background' (2010: 173). This book therefore also needs to be read as the latest stage of a decade of key work bridging sociolinguistics and linguistic anthropology, drawing attention to the need to understand local language practices such as grassroots literacy not only in terms of their immediate surrounds but also in terms of how they got there, historically and spatially. *Ethnography, Superdiversity and Linguistic Landscapes* on the one hand takes Blommaert's work forward though this detailed examination of the LL of Oud-Berchem, an inner-city neighbourhood in Antwerp, while on the other hand it takes work in LLs – and discourse analysis and sociolinguistics more generally – forward by insisting on the importance of the ethnographic understanding of textual complexities.

Alastair Pennycook
Brian Morgan
Ryuko Kubota

Note

(1) Jens Normann Jørgensen died on 29th May, 2013, during the writing of this preface. His inspirational work has had an enormous impact on the work of many of us in the fields of sociolinguistics and education. A close collaborator of Jan Blommaert, too, he will be very sadly missed.

References

Blommaert, J. (2005) *Discourse: A Critical Introduction*. Cambridge: Cambridge University Press.

Blommaert, J. (2008) *Grassroots Literacy: Writing, Identity and voice in Central Africa*. London: Routledge.

Blommaert, J. (2010) *The Sociolinguistics of Globalization*. Cambridge: Cambridge University Press.

Bourdieu, P. (1991) *Language and Symbolic Power*. Oxford: Polity Press.

Clarke, M.A. (2003) *A Place to Stand: Essays for Educators in Troubled Times*. Ann Arbor: University of Michigan Press.

Coulmas, F. (2009) Linguistic landscaping and the seed of the public sphere. In E. Shohamy and D. Gorter (eds) *Linguistic Landscape: Expanding the Scenery*. London: Routledge, 13–24.

Coupland, N. (2013) Welsh tea: The centring and decentring of Wales and the Welsh language. In S. Pietikäinen and H. Kelly Holmes (eds) *Multilingualism and the Periphery* (pp. 133–153). Oxford: Oxford University Press.

Jaffe, A. and Oliva, C. (2013) Linguistic creativity in Corsican tourist context. In S. Pietikäinen and H. Kelly Holmes (eds) *Multilingualism and the Periphery* (pp. 95–117). Oxford: Oxford University Press.

Jaworski, A. and Thurlow, A. (2013) The (de-)centring spaces of airports: Framing mobility and multilingualism. In S. Pietikäinen and H. Kelly Holmes (eds) *Multilingualism and the Periphery* (pp. 154–198). Oxford: Oxford University Press.

Jørgensen, J.N. (2008) Urban wall writing. *International Journal of Multilingualism* 5 (3), 237–252.

Larsen-Freeman, D. (2012) Complexity theory. In S.M. Gass and A. Mackey (eds) *The Routledge Handbook of Second Language Acquisition* (pp. 73–87). New York: Routledge.

Malinowski, D. (2009) Authorship in the linguistic landscape: A multimodal-performative view. In E. Shohamy and D. Gorter (eds) *Linguistic Landscape: Expanding the Scenery* (pp. 107–125). London: Routledge.

Pennycook, A. (2009) Linguistic landscapes and the transgressive semiotics of graffiti. In E. Shohamy and D. Gorter (eds) *Linguistic Landscape: Expanding the Scenery* (pp. 302–312). London: Routledge.

Pennycook, A. (2010) Spatial narratives: Graffscapes and city souls. In A. Jaworski and C. Thurlow (eds) *Semiotic Landscapes: Language, Image, Space* (pp. 137–150). London: Continuum.

Scollon, R. and Scollon, S.W. (2003) *Discourses in Place: Language in the Material World*. London: Routledge.

Shohamy, E. and Gorter, D. (2009) Introduction. In E. Shohamy and D. Gorter (eds) *Linguistic Landscape: Expanding the Scenery* (pp. 1–10). London: Routledge.

van Lier, L. (2004) *The Ecology and Semiotics of Language Learning: A Sociocultural Perspective.* Boston: Springer.

van Lier, L. (2011) Language learning: An ecological-semiotic approach. In E. Hinkel (ed.) *Handbook of Research in Second Language Teaching and Learning* (vol. 2, pp. 383–394). New York: Routledge.

1 Introduction: New Sociolinguistic Landscapes

These days, sociolinguists do not just walk around the world carrying field notebooks and sound recording equipment; they also carry digital photo cameras with which they take snapshots of what has, in the meantime, become known as 'linguistic landscapes'. Such landscapes capture the presence of publicly visible bits of written language: billboards, road and safety signs, shop signs, graffiti and all sorts of other inscriptions in the public space, both professionally produced and grassroots. The locus where such landscapes are being documented is usually the late-modern, globalized city: a densely multilingual environment in which publicly visible written language documents the presence of a wide variety of (linguistically identifiable) groups of people (e.g. Backhaus, 2007; Barni, 2008; Barni & Bagna, 2008; Barni & Extra, 2008; Ben-Rafael *et al.*, 2006; Coupland & Garrett, 2010; Gorter, 2006; Jaworski, 2010; Landry & Bourhis, 1997; Lin, 2009; Shohamy & Gorter, 2009). Excursions into less urban and more peri-urban or rural spaces are rare, even though they occur and yield stimulating results (e.g. Juffermans, 2010; Stroud & Mpendukana, 2009; Wang, 2013; Juffermans also provides a broad spectre of signs in his analysis of The Gambia). In just about a decade, linguistic landscape studies (henceforth LLS) have gained their place on the shelves of the sociolinguistics workshop.

I welcome this development for several reasons. The first and most immediate reason is the sheer potential offered by LLS. This potential is *descriptive* as well as *analytical*. In descriptive terms, LLS considerably expand the range of sociolinguistic description from, typically, (groups of) speakers to *spaces*, the physical spaces in which such speakers dwell and in which they pick up and leave, so to speak, linguistic deposits, 'waste', signposts and roadmaps. Note that older sociolinguistic traditions such as dialectology *also* included space into their object – the typical scholarly product of dialectology was the dialect-geographical map. But space was a secondary concern in dialectology, as we shall discuss in greater detail below. The spaces of the dialect atlases were empty, unsemiotized spaces onto which speaking people were plotted. In LLS, space *itself* is the central object and concern, and this is an important extension of the traditional scope of sociolinguistics (see Stroud & Mpendukana, 2009).

I will elaborate this descriptive and analytical potential further in what follows; but before that, another important potential of LLS needs to be mentioned. I see LLS as one branch of sociolinguistics that could be of immense interdisciplinary value. The reason is the clear overlap between LLS and disciplines such as social geography, urban studies and the anthropology and sociology of diversity. The overlap is in the terrain covered by LLS: as said, space is now sociolinguistically thematized and examined, and the space covered by LLS is the same as that covered by several other disciplines. We have here an opportunity to show the relevance of sociolinguistic investigation, the ways in which attention to sociolinguistic aspects of space can contribute to better and more precise analyses of social space in general, of space as inhabited and invested by people. And the relevance we can have is sited in the potential of LLS, to which I can now return.

The descriptive potential is indeed quite formidable, for it comes with several quite interesting side effects, of which I shall briefly review some.

- One, LLS can act as a first-line sociolinguistic *diagnostic* of particular areas. It offers the fieldworker a relatively user-friendly toolkit for detecting the major features of sociolinguistic regimes in an area: monolingual or multilingual? And in the case of the latter, which languages are there? From such a quick and user-friendly diagnosis, one can move into more profound investigations into the sociolinguistic regime, and feed those back to the diagnosis. This book hopes to provide an example of that.
- Two, given this diagnostic value, LLS will at the very least protect researchers from major errors – as when an area identified as the research target proves not to offer the multilingualism one had expected to meet there, on the basis of an exploration of published sources or less reliable travelers' accounts. Thus, LLS can be used as an excellent tool for explorative fieldwork and will enhance the realism of research proposals. The potential is thus also practical.
- Three, and more fundamentally, LLS compels sociolinguists to pay more attention to *literacy*, the different forms and shapes of literacy displayed in public spaces. This is blissful, for traditional sociolinguistics can thereby shed some of its historical bias towards spoken language forms and incorporate crucial sociolinguistic views developed in (the at present

rather parallel universe of) literacy studies. The specific place of literacy in sociolinguistic economies has traditionally been downplayed in mainstream textbooks. The unfortunate consequence of this is that important sociolinguistic features that can only, or most persuasively, be read off literacy artifacts have not been incorporated into considerations of the sociolinguistic system. In that sense, sociolinguistics has never really been *comprehensive* in my view.

- Finally, I will also try to show that LLS compel us towards *historicizing* sociolinguistic analysis. The arguments for that will be elaborated in the remainder of the book; I firmly believe that renewed and deepened LLS heralds the end of the dominance of a synchronic (or achronic) perspective in linguistics and sociolinguistics. More, in particular I intend to show how LLS can detect and interpret social change and transformation on several scale-levels, from the very rapid and immediate to the very slow and gradual ones. This could be an important contribution of LLS to other disciplines: we can detect indexes of change long before they become visible in statistics or other large-scale investigations.

The potential of LLS is not just descriptive; it is also analytical. While a 'light' version of LLS can act as a useful tool in the sense outlined above, a higher-octane version of it can do vastly more.

The reason for that is at first sight rather simple. Physical space is also social, cultural and political space: a space that offers, enables, triggers, invites, prescribes, proscribes, polices or enforces certain patterns of social behavior; a space that is never no-man's-land, but always *somebody's* space; a *historical* space, therefore, full of codes, expectations, norms and traditions; and a space of *power* controlled by, as well as controlling, people. We know all of that. Yet, it is not enough to merely exclaim this; it needs to be demonstrated and therefore requires careful and meticulous moves. The move from a physical to a social space (from dialectology to LLS, in other words) and from a synchronic to a historical space is not automatic and self-evident, but is precisely lodged in a deeper analysis of the linguistic landscape as indexing social, cultural and political patterns. The sociolinguistic diagnostic mentioned above can thus become a diagnostic of social, cultural and political *structures* inscribed in the linguistic landscape.

This I see as the greatest potential offered by LLS, and this will be the object of this book. The book has emerged out of an understanding of this fantastic potential, and of an awareness that this potential can only be realized when LLS are analytically deepened and theoretically matured – both points currently representing major weaknesses of the young discipline. I welcome LLS, therefore, also for another reason than the potential it offers: I welcome the analytical and theoretical challenges it offers us. It represents a genuine opportunity to improve our science. Through work on LLS, I believe we can make the whole of sociolinguistics better, more useful, more comprehensive and more persuasive, and to offer some relevant things to other disciplines in addition. This book aspires to offer some tentative lines into that task.

The range of issues we are required to address is both vast and complex. In what follows I shall engage with some of the major themes that demand attention, and I shall specify my own position in their regard.

Superdiversity

I must open with a sketch of the background for this work – the wider panorama in which we will locate and dissect linguistic landscapes. That wider panorama is a form of social, cultural, economic diversity for which Steven Vertovec coined the term 'superdiversity' – diversity within diversity, a tremendous increase in the texture of diversity in societies such as ours (Vertovec, 2007, 2010). This increase is the effect of two different but obviously connected forces, emerging at the same moment in history and profoundly affecting the ways in which people organize their lives.

The first force is the end of the Cold War. Since the early 1990s, the 'order' in the world has fundamentally changed. This 'order', during the Cold War, was quite clearly defined: people from one camp did not often or easily travel to or interact with people from the other camp; if they did that, it would be under severely conflictual circumstances, as refugee or dissident. The effects of that order included the fact that one would literally never see a car with, e.g. Bulgarian or Romanian license plates on Western European roads. Migration prior to the early 1990s was a well-regulated phenomenon, organized on a cross-national basis in such a way that the profiles of 'migrants' into Western European societies were rather clearly defined and predictable. Migration into Belgium, for instance, would include several waves reflecting agreements between governments about migration. First, people from Italy and other countries north of the Mediterranean would arrive; then people from Morocco and Turkey would be attracted. Migration was labor migration, and very little migration happened in other categories, such as asylum seeking.

The end of the Cold War changed the patterns of human mobility in the world, and one visual feature of that is that nowadays one can observe hundreds of vehicles with Bulgarian, Romanian, Lithuanian, Polish, Czech license plates on almost any highway in Western Europe. Another one would be the presence of students from the People's Republic of China on almost every university campus in the Western world. The robust boundaries that contained populations were all but erased, and in combination with growing instability in many parts of the world (not least in the former Warsaw Pact countries), massive new migrations were set in motion. Labor migration in the old fashion sense became less prominent; asylum seekers became, from the early 1990s onwards, the single biggest category of immigrants in Europe, and crises in the asylum systems have been endemic for about two decades now. In general, more people from more places migrated into more and different places and for more and different reasons and motives than before (Vertovec, 2010); and the outcome was an escalation of ethnic, social, cultural and economic diversity in societies almost everywhere. Unstable, highly volatile and unpredictable demographic and social patterns evolved, and they were further complicated by the second force behind superdiversity: the internet.

The world went online at more or less exactly the same moment as that of the end of the Soviet Union. In the early 1990s, the internet became a widely available infrastructure, and by the late 1990s Web 2.0 was there, offering a vast and unparalleled expansion of the means for exchanging long-distance information and for developing and maintaining translocal ties (documented early on by, e.g. Appadurai, 1996; Castells, 1996; Lash & Urry, 1994). Mobile phones became widespread at approximately the same time, and their effect was to detach possibilities for communication from fixed spaces, like the phone booth or the phone corner in the living room. So from the mid- to late-1990s onwards, communication patterns in the world changed dramatically, and with them the capacity to maintain virtual networks and communities, to circulate, produce and absorb information, and to engage in entirely new forms of social interaction, such as in social media and mass online gaming. The effects on how we lead our social and cultural lives are the object of an exploding literature, and while all sorts of questions can be asked about specific patterns of online conduct, the fact is that the impact of the internet and other communication technologies is fundamental and pervasive (see e.g. Davidson & Goldberg, 2010).

The interaction of these two forces – new and more complex forms of migration, and new and more complex forms of communication and knowledge circulation – has generated a situation in which two questions have become hard to answer: who is the Other? And who are We? The Other is now a category in constant flux, a moving target about whom very little can be presupposed; and as for the We, ourselves, our own lives have become vastly more complex and are now very differently organized, distributed over

online as well as offline sites and involving worlds of knowledge, information and communication that were simply unthinkable two decades ago.

This is superdiversity. It is driven by three keywords: mobility, complexity and unpredictability. The latter is of course a knowledge issue, which
pushes us to a perpetual revision and update of what we know about societies. This, I believe, is the paradigmatic impact of superdiversity: it questions
the foundations of our knowledge and assumptions about societies, how they
operate and function at all levels, from the lowest level of human face-to-face
communication all the way up to the highest levels of structure in the world
system. Interestingly, language appears to take a privileged place in defining
this paradigmatic impact; the reasons for that will be specified below, and
the privileged position of language as a tool for detecting features of superdiversity is the reason why I write this book.

Complexity

I have outlined the background against which we will have to operate
and set our work in this book. Let us now dig into some of the conceptual
tools needed for the work ahead of us. I will of course focus on language in
society, but while doing that I will also introduce themes that we share with
some of the other disciplines mentioned earlier.

I have for several years tried to address the effects of globalization on various aspects of the study of language in society, and this book can be seen as an
extension and deepening of earlier attempts: on discourse and discourse analysis (Blommaert, 2005b), on literacy and how to address it (Blommaert, 2008)
and on the sociolinguistic study of globalized environments (Blommaert,
2010). The central notion in these earlier attempts was *mobility*: I assumed (and
still assume) that thinking about language in society in terms of mobility is a
major theoretical effort, for it disrupts a very long tradition in which language,
along with other social and cultural features of people, was primarily imagined
as relatively fixed in time and space.

Disturbing mobility

A language or language variety was seen as something that 'belonged' to
a definable (and thus bounded) 'speech community'; that speech community
lived in one place at one time and, consequently, shared an immense amount
of contextual knowledge. That is why people understood each other: they
knew all the social and cultural diacritics valid in a stable sociolinguistic
community and could, thus, infer such contextual knowledge in interactions

with fellow members of that speech community. Roles and expectations were clear and well understood in such contexts – children had respect for elder people and so forth. And people reproduced patterns that were seen as anchored in a timeless tradition – the rules of language usage are what they are, because the rules of society are what they are (for a critique, see Rampton, 1998). Social and linguistic features were members of separate categories, between which stable and linear correlations could be established.

Labov's (1963) study of Martha's Vineyard (not by coincidence an *island*, I believe) can serve as a prototype of such assumptions of fixedness and stability; the work of Joshua Fishman on macro-sociolinguistics equally articulates these assumptions (Fishman, 1972; Fishman & Garcia, 2010; see also Williams, 1992, for a critique).

Gumperz and Hymes (1972), however, quickly destabilized these assumptions, and they did so with one apparently simple theoretical intervention: they defined social and linguistic features not as separate-but-connected, but as *dialectic*, i.e. co-constructive and, hence, *dynamic*. Concretely: the reiteration of specific patterns of language usage – say, the use of 'yes sir' as an answer in a hierarchical speech situation – creates a social structure (hierarchy), which in turn begins to exert a compelling effect on subsequent similar speech situations. It has become a 'rule' or a 'norm' and so becomes an ideologically saturated behavioral expectation; but such 'rules' or 'norms' have no abstract existence, they only have an existence in iterative communicative enactment. People need to perform such ideologically saturated forms of behavior – their behavior must be iterative in that sense – but small deviations from that 'rule' have the capacity to overrule the whole of norm-governed behavior. Saying 'yes sir' with a slow and dragging intonation, for instance, ('yeeees siiiiiiiir') can express irony and so entirely cancel the norm, and even become the beginning of an alternative norm.

The importance of this simple but fundamental change in perspective is massive, for it introduced a dimension of contingency and complexity into sociolinguistics that defied the static correlational orthodoxies. Deviations from norms, for instance, can now be the effect of a whole range of factors, and it is impossible to make an a priori choice for any of them. The dragging intonation in our example above can be the result of intentional subversion; but it can also be the effect of degrees of 'membership' in speech communities – whether or not one 'fully' knows the rules of the sociolinguistic game. So, simple correlations do not work anymore, they need to be established by means of ethnographic examination. In my work, this issue of 'full membership' and 'full knowledge' – an issue of inequality – has consistently figured as one of the big questions. And I realized that mobility in the context of globalization and superdiversity led to more and more cases and situations in which 'full membership' and 'full knowledge' were simply not there; there were, to put it simply, way too many exceptions to the rule to leave the rule itself unchallenged.

Mobility, for me and many others then, has three major methodological effects: (a) it creates a degree of unpredictability in what we observe; (b) we can only solve this unpredictability by close ethnographic inspection of the minutiae of what happens in communication; and (c) by keeping in mind the intrinsic limitations of our current methodological and theoretical vocabulary – thus, by accepting the need for new images, metaphors and notions to cover adequately what we observe. The challenge of mobility is paradigmatic, not superficial (cf also Blackledge & Creese, 2010; Jaworski & Thurlow, 2010; Jørgensen *et al.*, 2011; Møller & Jørgensen, 2011; Pennycook, 2010, 2012; Rampton, 2006; Stroud & Mpendukana, 2009; Weber & Horner, 2012).

The paradigmatic nature of the challenge is hard to escape when one addresses the many new forms of multilingual communicative behavior that seem to characterize the present world, and for which scholars have developed terms such as 'languaging', 'polylanguaging', 'crossing', 'metrolingualism', 'transidomatic practices' and so forth (Blommaert & Rampton, 2011, provide a survey). In superdiverse environments (both online and offline), people appear to take any linguistic and communicative resource available to them – a broad range, typically, in superdiverse contexts – and blend them into hugely complex linguistic and semiotic forms. Old and established terms such as 'codeswitching', and indeed even 'multilingualism', appear to rapidly exhaust the limits of their descriptive and explanatory power in the face of such highly complex 'blends' (cf Backus, 2012; Creese & Blackledge, 2010; Sharma & Rampton, 2011). And not only that: the question where the 'stuff' that goes into the blend comes from, how it has been acquired, and what kind of 'competence' it represents, is equally difficult to answer. Contemporary repertoires are tremendously complex, dynamic and unstable, and *not* predicated on the forms of knowledge-of-language one customarily assumes, since Chomsky, with regard to language (Blommaert & Backus, 2012).

Superdiversity, thus, seems to add layer upon layer of complexity to sociolinguistic issues. Not much of what we were accustomed to methodologically and theoretically seems to fit the dense and highly unstable forms of hybridity and multimodality we encounter in fieldwork data nowadays. Patching up will not solve the problem; fundamental rethinking is required.

Complexity: Theory as inspiration

In the mid-1980s, I keenly devoured popularizing books on relativity theory, quantum physics and chaos theory. Two books stood out as highlights in reading: Waddington's (1977) *Tools for Thought* about complex systems, and, especially, Prigogine and Stengers' (1984) classic *Order out of Chaos*. The fact that the latter book was written by two fellow Belgians, one a Nobel Prize winner and the other a distinguished philosopher, no doubt contributed to the eagerness with which I read and discussed their book. Looking back, I have severely underestimated the depth of the effect of these books on my view of things.

Both books introduced (at the time) entirely new ways of thinking about nature, the universe and society; and both books emphasized the crucial role of (and perpetual need for!) fantasy and imagination, 'the conceptual creativeness of scientific activity' (Prigogine & Stengers, 1984: 18). When certain theories or methods do not work, one option is to disqualify the data that brought the theoretical machinery to a standstill. Another one, of course, and the one advocated by Prigogine and Stengers (1984) as well as by Waddington (1977), is to understand this failure as owing to an as yet unperceived and thus unknown fundamental feature of reality, and theoretical and methodological innovation is needed in order to identify, know and understand that feature. I liked that idea.

The books introduced a world of complex systems: systems that were open and unfinished, in and on which several apparently unrelated forces operated simultaneously but without being centrally controlled or planned, so to speak. In such systems, change was endemic and perpetual, because of two different dynamics: interaction with other systems (an external factor), and intra-system dynamics and change affected by such exchanges with others, but also operating autonomously (an internal factor). Consequently, no two interactions between systems were identical, because the different systems would have changed by the time they entered into the next ('identical') interaction. Repeating a process never makes it identical to the first one, since repetition itself is a factor of change. The authors also stressed the importance of contingency and accident – the 'stochastic' side of nature. General patterns can be disrupted by infinitely small deviations – things that would belong to statistical 'error margins' can be more crucial in understanding change than large 'average' patterns. And they emphasized the non-unified character of almost any system, the fact that any system can and does contain forces and counterforces, dominant forces and 'rebellious' ones.

Particularly inspiring, of course, was the conclusion that chaos is not an absence of order but a *specific form of order*, characterized, intriguingly, by the increased interaction, interdependence and hence *coherence* between different parts of a system. And the assumption that such general chaotic patterns can be found at every scale level – authors usually distinguish the microscopic world from the macroscopic one – was both challenging and productive as well. Finally, but more speculatively, the notion of entropy can be useful to keep in mind: systems inevitably develop entropy, a loss of the energy that characterizes their non-equilibrium state, and tend to develop towards uniformity. Their internal pattern of change, in other words, tends towards homogeneity and the reduction of the intense energy of diversity.

Those ideas are decades old by now, and many of them have become common sense. But not, I observe with regret, in sociolinguistics and many other branches of the human and social sciences, nor in public policy. They have more influence and are much better understood in New Age movements than in the EU Commission or in any department of sociolinguistics, and this is a pity.[1] In my own work, they were often a *basso continuo*, a presence below-the-radar rarely spelled out explicitly; perhaps it is time now to do so.

But before I do, an important qualification must be made. I am not, and have no intention, of becoming an 'expert' in what is now called chaos theory or complexity theory. And I will not 'use' or 'apply' chaos theory to sociolinguistic phenomena; whoever intends to read this book as a chaos-theoretical sociolinguistic study should abandon that attempt right now. I use chaos theory as a *source of inspiration*, a reservoir of alternative images and metaphors that can help me on my way to re-imagining sociolinguistic phenomena – not a fixed and closed doctrine that I must follow in order to do my work well. Several perversions of chaos theory will consequently pollute my approach; I am aware of them and they are *needed*. I use complexity as a *perspective*, not as a compulsory vocabulary or theoretical template. It offers me a *freedom to imagine*, not an obligation to submit.

Complex sociolinguistics

In earlier work, I developed several notions that could be profitably recycled, and could gain clarity, by being put in a more coherent complexity perspective. Let me summarize and review them; I will do that in the form of a series of theoretical statements that will inform the remainder of the book.

(1) A sociolinguistic system is a *complex system* characterized by internal and external forces of perpetual change, operating simultaneously and in unpredictable mutual relationships. It is, therefore, always dynamic, never finished, never bounded, and never completely and definitively describable either. By the time we have finished our description, the system will have changed. As for the notion of 'sociolinguistic system', it simply stands for any set of systemic – regular, recurrent, nonrandom – interactions between sociolinguistic objects at any level of social structure.

(2) Sociolinguistic systems are *not unified* either. In earlier work, I used the notion of *polycentricity* to identify the fragmentation and the interactions between fragments of a sociolinguistic system. A sociolinguistic system is always a 'system of systems', characterized by different *scale levels* – the individual is a system, his/her peer group is one, his/her age category another and so on. We move from the smallest 'microscopic' or 'nano-sociolinguistic' level (Parkin, 2013), to the highest 'macroscopic' scale level. Centers in a polycentric system typically occupy specific scale levels and operate as foci of *normativity*, that is, of ordered indexicalities (Silverstein, 2003; Blommaert, 2005b). The norms valid in a small peer group are different from those operating on the same individuals in a school context, for instance.

(3) Sociolinguistic systems are characterized by *mobility*: in the constant interaction within and between systems, elements move across centers and scale levels. In such forms of mobility, the characteristics of the elements change: language varieties that have a high value here, can lose that value easily by moving into another 'field of force', so to speak – another sociolinguistic system. Concretely, an accent in English that bears middle-class prestige in Nairobi can be turned into a stigmatized immigrant accent in London (cf Blommaert, 2010).

(4) The reason for such changes is *historical*: the value and function of particular aspects of a sociolinguistic system are the outcome of historical processes of becoming. At the lowest level of language, word meanings are 'conventional', that is 'historically entrenched as meaning x or y'. Historicity creates recognizability, grounded in indexical attributions: I hear x, and I recognize it as conventionally and indexically meaning y. This also counts for higher-order levels such as genres, styles, discourse traditions and other forms of intertextuality and interdiscursivity (Blommaert, 2005b; Agha, 2007).

(5) In a complex system, we will encounter *different historicities* and different *speeds of change* in interaction with each other, collapsing in synchronic moments of occurrence. Long histories – the kind of history that shaped 'English', for instance – are blended with shorter histories, such as the one that produced HipHop jargon, for instance. I called this 'layered simultaneity' in earlier work (Blommaert, 2005b: 126): the fact that in communication, resources are used that have fundamentally different historicities and therefore fundamentally different indexical loads. The process of lumping them together, and so eliding the different historicities inscribed in them, I called 'synchronization'. Every synchronic act of communication is a moment in which we synchronize materials that each carry very different historical indexicalities, an effect of the intrinsic polycentricity that characterizes sociolinguistic systems.

(6) I made the previous statement years ago as a general typification of discourse, from individual utterance to text and discourse complex. I am now ready to make the same statement with respect to larger units as well, as a typification of entire zones of communication and of communicative systems in general. One of the reasons is that I am now, perhaps too boldly, inclined to accept *fractal recursivity* as a rule: the fact that phenomena occurring on one scale level also resonate at different scale levels (Irvine & Gal, 2000). The intrinsic hybridity of utterances (something, of course, introduced by Bakhtin a long time ago) is an effect of interactions within a much larger polycentric system.

(7) The synchronization mentioned earlier is an act of interpretation in which the different historical layers of meaning are folded into one 'synchronic' set of meanings. This is a reduction of complexity, and every form of interpretation can thus be seen as grounded in a reduction of the complex layers of meaning contained in utterances and events – a form of *entropy*, in a sense. People appear to have a very strong tendency to avoid or reduce complexity, and popular 'monoglot' language ideologies (Silverstein, 1996), as well as 'homogeneistic' language and culture policies (Blommaert & Verschueren, 1998), can exemplify this tendency. While the default tendencies of the system are towards entropy – uniformity, standardization, homogenization – the perpetual 'chaotic' dynamics of the system prevent this finite state. In sociolinguistic systems, we are likely to always encounter tensions between tendencies towards uniformity and tendencies towards heterogeneity. In fact, this tension may characterize much of contemporary social and cultural life (see Blommaert & Varis, 2012).

(8) In line with the previous remarks, change at one level also creates effects at other levels. Every instance of change is at least potentially *systemic*, since changes in one segment of the system have repercussions on other segments of that system. A simple example is the way in which parents can be influenced by their teenage children's internet gaming jargon and effectively adopt it in their own speech, even when these parents themselves never performed any online gaming in their lives. A change in one segment (the teenager child) affects other segments (his/her parents), and is provoked by higher-scale features (the jargon of online gaming communities). Similarly, in an argument I developed in Blommaert (2008), the generalized spread of keyboard literacy in certain parts of the world devalues longhand writing – the default form of literacy in less prosperous (segments of) societies.

(9) The latter remark has a methodological consequence. The loci of macroscopic change can be microscopic and unpredictable; large scale change

can be triggered by individual contingencies or recurrences of seemingly insignificant deviations. A jurisprudence-driven legal system is a good illustration: a single highly contingent ruling by a judge can change the whole system of legislation on related issues. This means that microscopic and detailed investigation of cases – ethnography, in other words – is perhaps the most immediately useful methodology for investigating systemic sociolinguistic aspects (cf also Blommaert & Rampton, 2011; Rampton, 2006). The precise *direction* of change is unpredictable as well because of the unpredictability of the other factors. We know that systems change irreversibly – we know, thus, that there is a *vector* of change – but what exactly the outcome of change will be is hard to determine. We can *believe* in a certain direction of change; but we will not necessarily see it happen. The history of language planning across the globe is replete with unexpected (and often unwelcome and unhappy) outcomes. Nonlinear effects are frequent and important.

(10) In view of all this, the task of analysis is not to reduce complexity – to reiterate, in other words, the synchronization of everyday understanding – but to demonstrate complexity, to unfold the complex and multifiliar features and their various different origins that are contained in synchronized moments of understanding. Recognizing that the synchrony of linguistics and sociolinguistics (the so-called 'Saussurean synchrony') is, in actual fact, an ideologically plied habit of synchronization, evidently destroys that synchrony.

I realize that all of these points sound rather abstract and perhaps daunting; I can reassure my readers, however, that they merely summarize insights repeatedly established in what amounts to a tower of sociolinguistic and linguistic-anthropological literature by now. I must also remind the reader once more that the list of points is *not* a complexity theory of sociolinguistics; it is merely a list of theoretical assumptions that I will use throughout this book, and which perhaps could be applied elsewhere as well. The terms in which I have couched my points are merely there because they enable me to imagine the sociolinguistics of superdiversity as organized on an entirely different footing from that which characterized the Fishmanian and Labovian sociolinguistic world. In fact, several of the points flatly contradict some of the most common assumptions in the study of language in society – the boundedness of speech communities, the stability, linearity and even predictable nature of sociolinguistic variation; the linear nature of linguistic and sociolinguistic evolution; the autonomy and boundedness of language itself, and so forth (cf Makoni & Pennycook, 2007, for a discussion). They have now been replaced by a default image of openness, dynamics, multifiliar and nonlinear development, unpredictability – what used to be considered deviant and abnormal has become, in this perspective, normal.

If superdiversity offers us a paradigmatic challenge, it is because we now see that the fundamental features of reality have changed; our imagery of such a reality needs to be adjusted accordingly. The price we have to pay for that is the cosy familiarity of a habituated worldview, and the clarity and user-friendliness of the paradigmatic terms in which that worldview was translated.

Chronicles of Complexity

I have outlined the conditions of superdiversity in which I will situate my work; and I have sketched my perspective on sociolinguistic complexity, defining the theoretical parameters within which I intend to work. Let me now turn to the story to be told in this book.

The central argument in this book is that linguistic landscaping research can be useful in illuminating and explaining the complex structures of superdiverse sociolinguistic systems. LLS can, thus, be turned into a tool for dissecting the various forms of sociolinguistic complexity that characterize our contemporary societies. But there are conditions that need to be met before LLS can do that.

In line with the theoretical and methodological principles given in the previous section, LLS needs to be brought within the orbit of ethnography. Just like an ethnography of face-to-face interaction, LLS needs to become the detailed study of situated signs-in-public-space, aimed at identifying the fine fabric of their structure and function in constant interaction with several layers of context (see e.g. Rampton, 2011; Hymes, 1972, provides an early source of inspiration here). The various historical layers encapsulated in signs need to be unpacked, and their precise role in the semiotization of space needs to be established. If we claim that it is through semiotic activity that physical space is turned into social, cultural and political space, we need to understand how exactly these processes of semiotization operate.

Chapters 2 and 3 will address crucial aspects of an ethnographic theory of linguistic landscapes, drawing inspiration from the work of Ron and Suzie Scollon and Gunther Kress. Chapter 2, an essay called 'Historical bodies and historical space', starts from the problem of synchronic 'snapshot' analysis, and addresses the ways in which semiotic activity – the use of signs – provides a fundamental historical dimension to space, to which complexes of 'recognizability' can be attached. Signs turn spaces into specific loci filled with expectations as to codes of conduct, meaning/making practices and forms of interpretation. And the use of such semiotized spaces – by means of processes of informal learning called 'enskilment' – shows how a historicized space also turns bodies into historicized actors-in-space. This theme is taken further in Chapter 3, 'Semiotic and spatial scope', where the specific functions of signs in semiotized space are being discussed. We will see that signs demarcate spaces, cutting them up in precisely circumscribed zones in which identities are being defined and enacted, forms of authority can be exerted, ownership and entitlement can be articulated – a complex range of social, cultural and political effects results from the semiotization of space.

These two chapters shape some basic understandings about what signs do in space, how space becomes a non-neutral (even agentive) zone in which *specific* and *ordered* identities, actions and meanings can be generated. The general drift of my argument is to see semiotized space as a material force in social, cultural and political life, something we ourselves have shaped as a meaningful system-of-meanings (a sociolinguistic system in other words) and that never stops acting as a compelling force on our everyday conduct. Two major insights should be culled from these chapters: that public space can be seen as a sociolinguistic system of a particular scale level – a set of nonrandom interactions between sociolinguistic objects – and that detecting the features of that system requires detailed attention to both the microscopic characteristics of single signs and the systemic relationships between signs. These two insights are fundamental, and they will underlie the next steps I shall take in this book.

These next steps consist of a detailed analysis of one particular space: my own neighborhood in inner-city Berchem (Belgium). In the Chapters 4, 5 and 6, I intend to provide a deep study of this neighborhood, using the kind of LLS developed in the earlier chapters. The neighborhood has become distinctly superdiverse; it is an area where, over the past decades, several layers of migration have resulted in an extremely multilingual and multicultural environment, with a very high level of instability. Groups that are present today can be gone tomorrow; premises serving as a lingerie shop can be turned into an Evangelical church in a matter of weeks. It is a prime illustration of the complexity characterizing superdiversity, even though this work of illustration is cumbersome and demanding.

The tactics I shall use in my attempt to describe and analyze the complexity of my superdiverse neighborhood revolve around a mixture of two methodological approaches: linguistic landscaping and longitudinal ethnographic observation. I have lived in this neighborhood for close to 20 years now, and I have been a direct witness to almost all of the transitions in the looks, structure and composition of the area over that period. Yet, a deep understanding of these processes of change is not something that evolves simply by 'being there'; most of my neighbors never noticed many of the specific developments and changes towards superdiversity I will describe here, and many of them would be surprised to read some of the stories told here.

This is where linguistic landscaping comes in. I have, since 2007, been collecting extensive corpora of linguistic landscaping material in my neighborhood. They have become a kind of longitudinal 'knowledge archive' supporting and scaffolding my observations (see Blommaert & Dong, 2010, for methodological explanations of this point). Combining my observations with the corpus of linguistic landscape data continually reveals that the signs in my neighborhood provide a far superior and more accurate diagnostic of changes and transformations in the neighborhood, compared with field notes or even interviews (let alone statistical surveys and other superficial forms of inquiry). The close analysis of the visual data can be fed into the longitudinal ethnographic observations, and vice versa, in a way that delivers a sharply articulated image of social processes over a span of time, identifying participants, their mutual forms of dependence and interaction, power differences, stages in processes of becoming and change, and so on. We can see the fine fabric of social processes, and their full complexity, by combining ethnographic observations with linguistic landscape data, and this book can be read as an elaborate argument in favor of such a methodological mix. LLS enriches ethnographic fieldwork, while ethnographic observations enrich LLS and bring out its full descriptive and explanatory potential. In such an integrated exercise, signs in public space document complexity – they are visual items that tell the story of the space in which they can be found, and clarify its structure.

This descriptive and explanatory potential resides in points made in Chapters 2 and 3: the fact that the semiotization of space turns space into a social, cultural and political habitat in which 'enskilled' people co-construct and perpetually enact the 'order' semiotically inscribed in that space. Thus, analytically, we can use a richly contextualized, ethnographically interpreted linguistic landscape as a synchronic and descriptive diagnostic of the complexities of the sociolinguistic system it circumscribes.

This synchronic-descriptive diagnostic will be the topic of Chapter 4, 'Signs, practices, people'. I will first give a brief contextual narrative on the neighborhood, and then engage in a 'cataloguing' exercise of the different users of space, the various kinds of signs we can find there, the activities and forms of organization we can read from such signs. I will start from the simplest aspect of traditional linguistic landscaping studies: counting languages, but work my way into more complex questions and more layered interpretations of signs, in line with the theoretical and methodological remarks made in Chapters 2 and 3.

We will quickly notice, however, that a purely synchronic study is impossible, for two reasons. One, a theoretical reason: every sign inevitably points towards its conditions of origins; in other words, we can 'read backwards' from signs into their histories of production – their sociolinguistic, semiotic and sociological conditions of origin. Every sign is also proleptic, it points forward to its potential uptake; investigating signs therefore makes it impossible to avoid an 'arrow of time' as Prigogine and Stengers (1984) called it. Two, an empirical reason: the diversity of signs in our synchronic snapshot already suggested historical layering in the linguistic landscape. The actual material shape of signs tells us that some are older than others, and that some are produced by established and self-confident communities, while others document the presence of recently arrived and weakly organized communities. Thus, the step towards historical interpretation is inevitable, and Chapter 5 addresses 'Change and transformation' in my neighborhood.

The neighborhood can now be seen as perpetually in motion, with layers upon layers of historically conditioned activity taking place, different speeds of change interacting and with anachronisms documenting the unfinished nature of certain transformations. In the end, the consolidated picture of the neighborhood is that of a non-unified, yet cohesive complex sociolinguistic system in which different forms of change occur simultaneously, at odds with the widespread public image of the neighborhood as simply 'deteriorating'. The fragmented and multifiliar nature of the neighborhood can be seen as a form of order, a complex of infrastructures for superdiversity held together by conviviality.

One of the conspicuous infrastructures for superdiversity in the neighborhood is the very numerous places of worship in the neighborhood – a feature that has spectacularly grown over the past handful of years. Chapter 6, 'The Vatican of the diaspora' zooms in on the role and function of churches in the neighborhood. In this chapter, the two methodological movements represented in Chapters 4 and 5 – a synchronic and a historical one – are integrated, and we follow the genesis and development of churches in the neighborhood through the kinds of signage they use and used. We can see how churches developed from largely 'ethnic' places of worship into open and ecumenical ones, and how such local phenomena display complex ties with other scale levels: some of the churches attract followers from a very wide area and operate as branches of fully globalized religious corporations.

Chapter 6 concludes the exploration of my neighborhood, and what remains to be done in my concluding Chapter 7 is to pull the various lines of the argument together and to reflect on some wider theoretical issues – the end of synchrony being the object on which I enjoy speculating most – as well as to offer a reappraisal of the potential relevance of LLS for adjacent disciplines.

The first thing I need to do, however, is to briefly introduce the terrain on which I shall work: my own neighborhood.

Introducing Berchem

Close to two decades ago, I moved with my family into Oud-Berchem, an inner-city neighborhood in the south-eastern part of Antwerp, part of the district of Berchem. Antwerp is located in the north of Belgium, in the part known as Flanders. Tourists may know it as the town where Rubens lived and worked, and as one of the world's biggest centers of the diamond trade; they may have admired its extraordinary cathedral and, afterwards, the rich choice of exquisite beers consumed in one of the many cosy cafés in the city.

By Belgian standards, Antwerp is a big and cosmopolitan city with about half a million inhabitants. Economically, it is a powerhouse. The Antwerp harbor is one of the world's largest ones; it employs many thousands of workers, and many thousands more are employed in the large industrial sites surrounding the harbor; trucks to and from the harbor perpetually congest the ring road around Antwerp, which is one of Europe's busiest highways. This economic preponderance does not mean that Antwerp is a city of prosperous people. The average income in the districts of Antwerp is lower than the Flemish average, and much lower than that of some of Antwerp's affluent suburbs. Unemployment is higher than the national average, and the harbor and access to other arteries of mobility have made Antwerp into a highly diverse city for centuries.

Antwerp has always counted a very large working class population employed in the harbor and adjacent industries, trade and commerce. It has consequently always counted large working class neighborhoods, and Oud-Berchem is one of those. From a rather village-like peripheral district of Antwerp in the early 20th century, it developed into a densely populated popular neighborhood after the second world war consisting of, mainly, lower-qualified laborers, clustering in the neighborhood surrounding the

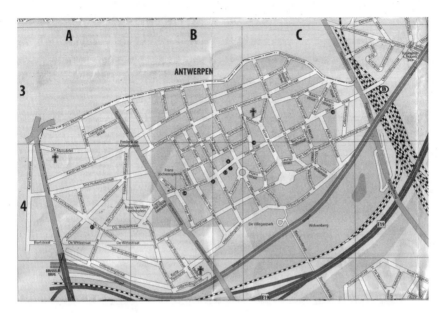

Figure 1.1 Map of Berchem
Source: City of Antwerp (public domain)

commercial axis of Statiestraat–Driekoningenstraat. These two joined streets, together about 1.2 kilometers long, connect the large railroad station (hence 'Statiestraat', 'Station Street') with an arterial road to the southern suburbs, and they still form the center of Oud-Berchem.

From the 1970s onwards, the neighborhood became a home for a large community of labor immigrants, mainly with Turkish origins. Until today, the Statiestraat–Driekoningenstraat area is known and perceived as the Turkish neighborhood of Antwerp. The Turkish immigrants bought property from the, by then, ageing Flemish working class, and the latter moved to the more remote districts of Antwerp where larger houses with gardens could be purchased.

The Turkish immigrants were followed, from the early- to mid-1990s on, by successive waves of immigrants from all over the world, often entering the country through the asylum procedure, and also quite often through clandestine and temporary immigration routes. Oud-Berchem is currently one of the Antwerp districts with the highest concentration of non-European immigrants, with a notable concentration of asylum seekers, and the central axis of the neighborhood, the Statiestraat–Driekoningenstraat, reflects this. Immigrants from all corners of the earth have opened shops, hair salons, cafés and restaurants there, visibly underscoring the superdiverse character of the neighborhood.

Figure 1.2 General view of Statiestraat

At the same time, Oud-Berchem has a higher than average unemployment rate, especially among younger immigrant men, and the average income is lower than the Antwerp average as well. This, too, is visible in the Statiestraat–Driekoningenstraat. The number of vacant commercial premises is high at any time, investments in improving the existing shops are low and older local Flemish people would often lament the disappearance of Flemish-owned commercial enterprise from the street (often called 'the better shops', in contradistinction with the foreign-operated groceries, hair salons, superettes, night shops and internet shops).

In terms of mobility and accessibility, Oud-Berchem offers several important assets. As mentioned, a major commuter railway station offers connections to almost every part of Belgium as well as to The Netherlands. A direct train ride to Brussels takes less than half an hour. The Antwerp ring road connects to major highways to the north (Breda and from there Rotterdam, Utrecht, Amsterdam and the German Ruhrgebiet); south (Brussels, and from there on to the Ardennes, Luxemburg, France and from there to Southern Europe); east (Hasselt, Liège, Eindhoven and from there to Cologne and Düsseldorf); and west (the North Sea coast, Paris, Calais and from there to the UK). It is one of Europe's major switchboards for overland traffic. Oud-Berchem is situated along the single busiest part of the Antwerp ring road, with exits and entrances within minutes reach from the Statiestraat–Driekoningenstraat. Tram and bus services connect the neighborhood to most other parts of the city.

Owing to these mobility opportunities, as well as to relatively affordable real estate prices, the neighborhood has recently started to attract young, native double-income families, often highly qualified and politically left-of-center. These recent and more affluent Belgian immigrants have purchased the larger middle-class houses in the area, and they have brought along their mostly young children. This bohemian segment of the population has generated a demand for cultural hubs, satisfied by a couple of local cafés that now present live music, literary and political events, by a celebrity chef who runs a very successful restaurant in the Driekoningenstraat and by a cultural center that stages avant-garde theater and dance.

Thus, we can see a dimension of unplanned gentrification in an area which, other than that, would score quite low in all sorts of socio-economic categories. This gentrification, of course, accelerates and infuses processes of class stratification (and re-stratification) in the neighborhood, in which, as we shall see further on, younger and highly educated members the Turkish community play a crucial role. The gentrification of the area has a modest effect on the linguistic landscape too: houses owned by this new Belgian middle-class segment will have posters against the windows expressing left-of-center political concerns, such as mobility and pollution, next to posters announcing 'high-culture' events in the area – world music, theatre and classical music shows.

My family and I have always been active community members in this neighborhood, launching or joining various forms of grassroots activism, participating in neighborhood committees and public hearings, actively involved in the parents' council of the schools, co-organizing a wide range of events and so forth. Most of all, I am someone who walks around a lot and talks to anyone who cares to talk to me. My ethnographic engagement with this neighborhood, therefore, is in its most literal sense longitudinal and participant observation; it is, in fact 'ethnographic monitoring' in the most immediate sense of the term (Hymes, 1980; Van der Aa, 2012; Van der Aa & Blommaert, 2011). It has enabled me to witness and capture both the objective and the subjective features of the area, to participate in processes of change and transformation – and experience such processes, and to maintain an extensive network of contacts and resource people in the neighborhood. The neighborhood has been my learning environment for about two decades now.

I can only introduce this neighborhood in the most general and superficial terms here. A more detailed picture of it will emerge in the chapters to follow. We are now ready to embark on this journey of exploration.

Note

(1) I am being unfair here towards the very interesting attempts made by some people in our field to adapt complexity/chaos theory to linguistic and sociolinguistic phenomena; see e.g. Diane Larsen-Freeman's work on language learning (Larsen-Freeman, 1997). I also see the study of linguistic landscapes in the townships near Cape Town by Stroud and Mpendukana (2009) as an important precursor to some of the arguments developed in this book.

2 Historical Bodies and Historical Space

In this and the next chapter, I will offer some building blocks for an ethnographic theory of linguistic landscapes. As announced earlier, the core of this theoretical argument is to see space as a historically configured phenomenon and as an actor, as something that operates as a material force on human behavior performed in space. Space is not neutral in other words, and if it is our intention to provide a more robust footing for LLS, we need to provide a sharply delineated vision on how space is semiotized, and how it semiotizes what goes on within its orbit. In this chapter, I will begin by sketching our main obstacle in this exercise: the deeply anchored synchronic view that dominates sociolinguistics and other disciplines. This obstacle, however, can be cleared in a remarkably simple way, using some tools developed in the work of Ron and Suzie Scollon detailed here.

There is something inherently ambivalent about ethnography. On the one hand, it is undoubtedly the success story of anthropology *par excellence*. It is the only anthropological development that has made it into mainstream social science; it is treated with respect by scholars in fields as widely apart as linguistics, psychology and history. On the other hand, though, ethnography has always had a doubtful reputation as well. It was under-theorized, relied too heavily on subjectivity and consequently produced data that did not stand the tests of a more rigid interpretation of objectivity in science. While there is a respectable body of fundamental methodological reflection on ethnography (e.g. Fabian, 1983, 2001, 2008; Hymes, 1996), this body of theory is relatively recent and its insights have not made it into the mainstream yet. The upshot of this is that much of what comes under the label of ethnography (including textbook introductions to it) lacks theoretical and methodological sophistication and is exposed to the same age-old criticism – a nasty experience shared by many a PhD student who have tried to argue in favor of ethnography in his or her dissertation proposal.

Theoretically sophisticated ethnography is rare, and it takes an effort to discover it, because sometimes it is found in work that does not announce or present itself as 'typical' ethnography (the fieldwork-based monograph is still the 'typical' ethnographic product). The work of Ron and Suzie Scollon is a case in point. Much of their major works do not *look* like ethnography. There are no lengthy introductions about the fieldwork that was conducted, for instance, and the main drive of their work is to contribute to semiotics and discourse analysis. Yet, they systematically insisted on the ethnographic basis of their work (e.g. Scollon & Wong Scollon, 2009). And this chapter will argue that their work contains very useful, even momentous interventions in ethnographic theory and method. If we talk about sophisticated ethnography, the work of the Scollons certainly qualifies for inclusion into that category.

I will focus in particular on two efforts by the Scollons (*Nexus analysis* (2004) and *Discourses in place* (2003)), and I will try to show that both works contain and articulate a theoretical overture towards history – an overture I find of major importance for ethnographic theory and method. The works do that, respectively, by means of a theorization of embodiment in the notion of 'the historical body', and by a theorization of space as agentive and non-neutral. Taken together, these two interventions offer us key ingredients necessary for transcending the perpetual risk of localism and anecdotism in ethnography, by allowing ethnography to move from the uniquely situated events it describes, to structural and systemic regularities in interpretation. This has implications for ethnography, indeed, but also for a broader field of studies of human conduct, including linguistics and sociolinguistics. Before moving on to discuss the two interventions by the Scollons, I first need to formulate the problem more precisely.

The Problem of Synchrony

The main methodological problem of ethnography, identified three decades ago by Johannes Fabian (1983), can be summarized as follows. Ethnography, typically, depends on data drawn from a bounded set of human encounters in real space and time. The ethnographer and his/her 'informant' interact, like all humans, in a contextually specific space–time that (as decades of research in pragmatics have taught us) defines the outcome of such interactions. The outcome is, typically, an epistemically genred collection of texts: recordings, field notes, and later a published paper or a monograph. Ethnographers walk away from the field with a collection of such texts, and these texts bear witness to the contextual conditions under which they were constructed. Concretely: phonetic descriptions of a language can differ when the informant misses both front teeth from when the informant has a fully intact set of them. It will also differ when the ethnographer had access to a sophisticated digital recording device for collecting the data, from when he or she had to rely solely on one's ear and competence in the use of the phonetic alphabet. Or, a narrative account of a robbery will differ depending on whether the narrator was the victim, the perpetrator or a witness of the robbery. And, of course, it will differ when the ethnographer him- or herself was involved in such roles in the robbery. The point is that ethnography draws its data from real-world moments of intersubjective exchange in which the ethnographer and the informant are both sensitive to the contextual conditions of this exchange (see also Blommaert, 2005a; Bourdieu, 2004).

The problem is, however, that as soon as the ethnographer tries to present his or her findings as 'science' – as soon as the 'data' enter the genre-machines of academic writing, in other words – this fundamental contextual sharedness is erased and replaced by a discursively constructed distance between the ethnographer and his or her 'object'. The sharedness of time and space, of language and of event structure gives way to a unidirectional, textual relationship in which the ethnographer is no longer an *interlocutor* alongside the informant, but a detached, 'objective' voice who does not talk with the interlocutor but *about* him or her. This problem is particularly acute when the ethnographer tries to generalize, i.e. use his or her data to make claims of general validity, of the type 'the Bamileke are matrilinear'. Fabian observes how in such textual moves, the timeless present tense is preferred over a discourse that represents this knowledge as situational and context-dependent. He notes that 'the present tense "freezes" a society at the time of observation' (Fabian, 1983: 81) and detaches ethnographic knowledge from the dialogical and context-sensitive frame in which it was constructed. The shared time–space in which it emerged is erased and replaced by a timeless present – something that Fabian calls the 'denial of coevalness' and identifies as a major epistemological problem hampering any ethnographic claim to general validity and generalization (see also Bourdieu, 2004).

This introduction of the timeless present is, of course, a widespread practice in the textual politics of scientific generalization and abstraction. It is central to what is known as 'synchronic' analysis in structural linguistics, mainstream sociolinguistics and discourse analysis, structuralist and functionalist anthropology and so forth. And in all of these disciplines, we encounter the same fundamental epistemological problem: as soon as scholars try to address structural or systemic features of a society, they have to shift from real time into abstract time, they have to extract features of dynamic lived experience and place them at a timeless, static plane of general validity. Whatever makes data social and cultural – their situatedness in social and cultural processes and histories – disappears and is replaced by 'laws' and 'rules' that appear to have a validity that is not contextually sensitive.

We are familiar with this move in structural linguistics, where notably the development of modern phonology in the early 20th century made 'synchrony' into the level at which scientific generalization of linguistic facts needed to be made. Michael Silverstein concisely summarizes this move as follows:

> Late in the 19th century, linguistics as a field transformed itself from a science focused on language change, the generalizations based on comparative and historical Indo-European, Semitic, Finno-Ugric, etc. At the center of such change was "phonetic law," and in seeking the causes for the "exceptionlessness" of phonetic changes, scholars went both to the phonetics laboratory and to the dialectological and "exotic language" field. The important results of such study, certainly achieved by the 1920s, were: the postulation (or "discovery") of the phonemic principle of abstract, immanent classes of sound realized variably in actual phonetic articulation and audition; and the *synchronicization* of linguistic theory as the theory of phonological structure involving structured relationships among the abstract sounds or phonological segments of any language, a syntagmatic and paradigmatic structure of categories of sound. (Silverstein, 2009: 14–15)

In this new modern linguistics, sound *change* was replaced by sound *replacement*. For people such as Bloomfield, this discovery of 'elementary particles' (phonemes) and of synchrony as the level of linguistic abstraction was cause to claim fully scientific status for linguistics (Silverstein, 2009: 15). Science, for him and many others in the heyday of structuralism, was the art of generalization, of identifying the immobile, non-dynamic, non-contextual, non-stochastic facts of language and social life. And this was done, precisely, by the elision of real time and real space from the purview of analysis. Analysis was synchronic, and to the extent that it was diachronic, the diachronicity of it rested on a sequenced juxtaposition and comparison of solidly synchronic states of affairs (Meeuwis & Brisard, 1993). Such diachronicity, in short, was not (and can never be) *historical*. To go by the words of Edwin Ardener commenting on the Neogrammarian approach:

> The grandeur of the Neogrammarian model for historical linguistics literally left nothing more to be said. This grandeur lay in its perfect generativeness. It did not, however, generate history. (Ardener, 1971: 227)

History is time filled with and defined by social and cultural actions, it is not just chronology on which events have been plotted. A lot of historical linguistics is in that sense *chronological* linguistics, not historical at all. Time in itself does not inform us about social systems, about patterns and structures of human organization. What can, historically, be seen as systemic or structural features (i.e. features that define a particular social system in a particular period) becomes in this chronological and synchronic paradigm converted into permanencies and hence into essences. Synchronicity, therefore, inevitably contains the seeds of essentialism.

The way to escape this trap is, one could argue, relatively simple: reintroduce history as a real category of analysis. The simplicity is deceptive of course, for what is required is a toolkit of concepts that are *intrinsically* historical; that is: concepts whose very nature and direction point towards connections between the past and the present in terms of *social* activities – concepts, in short, that define and explain synchronic social events in terms of their histories of becoming as social events. This is where we need to turn to the Scollons.

Historical Bodies in Historical Space

Our branches of scholarship already have a number of such intrinsically historical concepts. Terms such as intertextuality, interdiscursivity and entextualization, especially in their rich Bakhtinian interpretation, explain the textual present in relation to textual histories – not just histories of textual 'stuff', but also histories of use, abuse and evaluation of textual materials (e.g. Bauman & Briggs, 1990; Blommaert, 2005b; Fairclough, 1992; Silverstein, 2005; Silverstein & Urban, 1996; see, Johnstone, 2008: Chapter 5 for a survey and discussion). Whenever we use a term such as 'bitch' in relation to a female subject, we are not only introducing a semantic history into this usage of the term – the transformation of the meaning of 'female dog' to 'unpleasant woman' – but also a pragmatic and metapragmatic indexical history of the term – the fact that this term is used as an insult and should, consequently, not generally be used in public and formal performances. The extension to include a pragmatic and metapragmatic dimension to intertextual processes introduces a whole gamut of contextual factors into the analysis of intertextual processes. It's not just about borrowing and re-using 'texts' in the traditional sense of the term, it's about reshaping, reordering, reframing the text from one social world of usage into another one.

Nexus analysis started from a reflection on intertextuality. For the Scollons, human semiotic action could only be observed at the moment of occurrence, but needed to be analyzed in terms of 'cycles of discourse' (Scollon & Wong Scollon, 2004: Chapter 2) – a term which Ron Scollon later replaced by 'discourse itineraries' (Scollon, 2008). Such itineraries are trajectories of 'resemiotization', something that in turn relied on the Scollons' fundamental insight that discourse was always mediated (Scollon, 2001) – it was never just 'text', but always human social action in a real world full of real people, objects and technologies. Consequently, intertextuality needs to be broadly understood, for 'the relationship of text to text, language to language, is not a direct relationship but is always mediated by the actions of social actors as well as through material objects in the world' (Scollon, 2008: 233). And whenever we use words, that use 'encapsulates or resemiotizes an extended historical itinerary of action, practice, narrative, authorization, certification, metonymization, objectivization and technologization or reification' (Scollon, 2008: 233). Changes in any of these processes and practices are changes to the discourse itself; even if the discourse itself remains apparently stable and unaltered, the material, social and cultural conditions under which it is produced and under which it emerges can change and affect what the discourse is and does. Discourse analysis, for the Scollons, revolves around the task 'to map such itineraries of relationships among text, action and the material world through what we call a "nexus analysis"' (Scollon, 2008: 233).

Such an analysis naturally shares a lot with Bakhtinian notions of intertextuality and chronotope; at the same time it broadens the scope of the analysis by focusing on the interplay of the social and the material work in relation to discourse. And while intertextuality in the work of Fairclough and others still mainly addresses purely textual objects, the objects defined by the Scollons – nexuses – display far more complexity. A nexus is an intersection in real time and space of three different 'aggregates of discourse':

> the *discourses in place*, some social arrangement by which people come together in social groups (a meeting, a conversation, a chance contact, a queue) – the *interaction order*, and the life experiences of the individual social actors – the *historical body*. (Scollon & Wong Scollon, 2004: 19)

Discourse, as social action, emerges out of the nexus of these three forces, and an analysis of discourse consequently needs to take all three into consideration. To many, of course, this move is enough to recategorize the Scollons as semioticians rather than as discourse analysts. For the Scollons themselves, the ambition was to develop:

a more general ethnographic theory and methodology which can be used to analyze the relationships between discourse and technology but also place this analysis in the broader context of the social, political and cultural issues of any particular time. (Scollon & Wong Scollon, 2004: 7)

Observe here how this ethnographic–theoretical ambition takes the methodological shape of *historical* analysis. So when the Scollons talk about an ethnographically situated object – human action and practice – this object is historically grounded and generated, and the features of the synchronic object must be understood as temporary outcomes of this historical process of becoming. The three aggregates of discourse are all historical dimensions of any synchronic social action, and their historicity lies in the fact that all three refer to histories of 'iterative' human action crystallizing into normative social patterns of conduct, expectation and evaluation – *traditions* in the anthropological sense of the term. Synchronic events, thus, display the traces of (and can only be understood by referring to) normative–traditional complexes of social action, resulting (in a very Bourdieuan sense) in habituated, 'normal' or 'normalized' codes for conduct. And these codes, then, are situated in three different areas: individual experience, skills and capacities (the historical body), social space (discourses in place) and patterned, ordered, genred interaction (the interaction order).

The notion of 'interaction order' is attributed to Goffman (Scollon & Wong Scollon, 2004: 22). Yet, the actual meaning of that term and its use in *Nexus analysis* is an amendment to Goffman's 'interaction order'. In order to see that we need to look at the two other notions: historical bodies and historical space.

We have seen above that the Scollons defined the historical body as 'the life experiences of the individual social actors'; somewhat more explicitly, they also described it as people's 'life experiences, their goals and purposes, and their unconscious ways of behaving and thinking' (Scollon & Wong Scollon, 2004: 46). Whenever people enter into social action, they bring along their own skills, experiences and competences, and this 'baggage', so to speak, conditions and constrains what they can do in social action. Historical bodies have been formed in particular social spaces and they represent, to use an older notion, the 'communicative competence' of people in such social spaces.

Thus a teacher has grown accustomed to the school system, the actual school building where s/he works, his/her colleagues, the curriculum, the teaching materials and infrastructure, the ways of professionally organizing his/her work, academic discourse, the students. Various processes intersected in this: there is formal learning, there is informal learning, particular patterns are acquired while others are just encountered, certain skills are permanent while others are transitory and so on. The end result of this, however, is that the teacher can enter a classroom and perform adequately – s/he knows exactly where the classroom is, what kinds of activities are expected there, and how to perform these activities adequately. The historical body of the teacher has been formed in such a way that s/he will be perceived as a teacher by others, and that most of the actual practices s/he performs can be habitual and routine. Precisely the habitual and routine character of these practices makes them – at a higher level of social structure – 'professional' (see Pachler et al., 2008 for illustrations).

There is a long tradition of speaking about such things in relation to the mind; the Scollons, however, locate them in the body. What is actually perceived, and acted upon semiotically by other people, is a body in a particular space. This body talks, and behind the talking one can suspect thinking; but it also moves, manipulates objects, displays particular stances (aggression, tenderness, care, seriousness, etc.). It is the Scollons' preference for material aspects of discourse that makes them choose the body rather than the mind as the locus for such individual experiences.

But by doing so they open up a whole range of issues for the social study of language: issues of learning and acquisition in the semiotic field, questions about the way we appear to know what we know about signs and meanings. Until now, such questions have dominantly been answered by reference to the mind as well. The questions raised by a notion such as the historical body, however, shift the debate away from the mind and into the field of embodied knowledge. The gradual process by means of which teachers, for instance, acquire the habitual and routine practices and the knowledge to perform them adequately, cannot just be seen as a process of 'learning' in the traditional sense of the term. It is rather a process of *enskillment*: the step-by-step development, in an apprentice mode, of cultural knowledge through skillful activities (Gieser, 2008; also, Ingold, 2000; Jackson, 1989). Shared kinesthetic experiences with social activities (and talking would be one of them) lead to shared understandings of such activities, and 'meaning or knowledge is discovered in the very process of imitating another person's movements' (Gieser, 2008: 300).

Consider now how the Scollons describe a sequence of actions in which a teacher hands a paper to the student. First, the teacher must approach the student with the paper, and the student needs to understand the proximity of the teacher and his/her holding the paper in a particular way, as the beginning of a 'handing-the-paper' sequence. Both participants need to know these bodily routines of physical proximity, direction of movement and manipulation of an object. Then:

> the paper itself is handed through a long and practiced set of micro-movements that are adjusted to the weight of the object and the timing of the movements of their hands toward each other. Any very small failure of this timing and these movements and the object falls. This can easily lead to the embarrassment of the student or the teacher having to reach down to the floor to regain control of the paper. (Scollon & Wong Scollon, 2004: 64)

Observe how this moment of complex physical-kinesic handling of the paper is *semiotic*: if it is done wrongly, embarrassment may ensue – there may be giggling from the class, blushing from the student and/or the teacher, muttered mutual apologies and so forth. The 'practiced set of micro-movements', therefore, is replete with semiotic signs and signals, and carries social risks and rewards (making it, of course, a *normative* set: things have to be done in a particular way). It is embodied cultural knowledge – movements and positions of the body that convey cultural information and have acquired the shape of routine skills. Such movements have been 'practiced', they have a measure of immediate recognizability and they induce particular frames of action and understanding for all the participants. Whenever the Scollons discuss the ways in which students get used to keyboard-and-screen handling in a virtual learning environment, or seating arrangement and attention organization in traditional ('panoptic') classrooms, they emphasize the minute details of bodily practices – as acquired, enskilled forms of social conduct in a learning environment.

Through the notion of the historical body, thus, we see how a connection is made between semiotics and embodiment. Participants in social action bring their real bodies into play, but their bodies are semiotically enskilled: their movements and positions are central to the production of meaning, and are organized around normative patterns of conduct. And they do this, as we have seen, in a real spatial arena too. They do this, in actual fact, in close interaction with a historical space; so let us consider that historical space now.

As *Discourses in place* (Scollon & Wong Scollon, 2003) makes abundantly clear, space is never a neutral canvass for the Scollons. The book is, in fact, one of the very rare profound and sophisticated problematizations of space in the field of sociolinguistics, and while the notion of 'discourses in place' re-emerges in *Nexus analysis*, as we have seen, the treatment of space in *Discourses in place* reads like a mature contribution to linguistic landscaping. While a lot of work of LLS hardly questions the space in which linguistic signs appear, *Discourses in place* develops a whole theory of signs in space ('geosemiotics'), revolving around notions such as 'emplacement' – the actual semiotic process that results from the specific ('syntagmatic') location of signs in the material world. A 'no smoking' sign has this restrictive meaning only in the space where the sign is placed. So while the sign itself has a latent meaning, its meaning only becomes an actual social and semiotic fact when it is emplaced in a particular space. It is then that the sign becomes consequential: someone smoking in the vicinity of that sign can now be seen as a transgressor, someone who violates a rule clearly inscribed in that space. Emplacement, thus, adds a dimension of spatial scope to semiotic processes: it points towards the elementary fact that communication always takes place in a spatial arena, and that this spatial arena imposes its own rules, possibilities and restrictions on communication. Space, in that sense, is an *actor* in sociolinguistic processes, not a human actor, but a social actor nevertheless (see also, Blommaert *et al.*, 2005; Stroud & Mpendukana, 2009; more on this in the next chapter).

It is very often a *normative* actor in sociolinguistic processes, and this is where history enters the picture. There are expectations – normative expectations – about relationships between signs and particular spaces. One expects certain signs in certain places: shop signs and publicity billboards in a shopping street, for instance, or train timetables in a railway station. We do not expect such timetables in a café or a restaurant. When signs are 'in place', so to speak, habitual interpretations of such signs can be made, because the signs fit almost ecologically into their spatial surroundings. When they are 'out of place', or 'transgressive' in the terminology of the Scollons (Scollon & Wong Scollon, 2003: 147), we need to perform additional interpretation work because a different kind of social signal has been given. In a shopping street, shop signs are in place, while graffiti is out of place. The former belong there, the latter does not, and its presence raises questions of ownership of the place, of legitimate use of the place, of the presence of 'deviant' groups of users in that place and so on. So we attach to particular places a whole array of objects, phenomena, activities, and we do that in a normative sense, that is: we do it in a way that shapes our expectations of 'normalcy' in such places. We expect the people sitting in a university lecturing hall to be students, and we expect their behavior to be that of students as well; we can have very flexible expectations with regard to what they wear and how they look, but we would have more restrictive expectations about the objects they bring into the lecturing hall (a student entering the hall with a shotgun would, for instance, be highly unexpected and, consequently, alarming). We also expect them to use certain types of speech and literacy resources during the lecture – and when all of that is in place, we feel that the lecture proceeded 'normally'.

It is *the connection between space and normative expectations*, between space and 'order', that makes space historical, for the normative expectations we attach to spaces have their feet in the history of social and spatial arrangements in any society. The fact that we have these clear and widely shared expectations about university lecturing rooms is not a synchronic phenomenon: it is something that belongs to the history of institutions. And getting acquainted to such histories is part of the processes of enskillment we discussed earlier. We have been enskilled in recognizing the nature of particular places, and we are able to act appropriately – that is 'normally' – in such places. We now enter a lecture hall and we know exactly what to do and how to do it; we are instantly tuned into the patterns of normative expectations that belong to that place – for instance, silence from the students as soon as the lecturing starts – and we react accordingly when transgressive signs are being produced (as when a student's mobile phone goes off, or someone walks into the hall with a shotgun). An 'interaction order' falls into place, literally, as soon as we have entered that place and the place has been mutually recognized as such-and-such a place. The historical bodies and the historical space now operate in terms of the same order.

The historical body is, thus, narrowly connected to historical spaces: we get enskilled in the use of social and physical space, and our bodies fall into shape (or out of shape) each time we enter or leave a certain space. This, I believe, is the core of the Scollons' insistence on language in the material world: the material world is a spatial world, a real material environment full of objects, technologies and signs, upon which we act semiotically. Human semiotic behavior, thus, is behavior in real space, in relation and with reference to real space. The nexus of the historical body and of discourses in place is a historical, normative nexus, in which both dialectically generate the conditions for communication, its potential and its restrictions.

The third element of the nexus triad, the 'interaction order', in that sense becomes something rather far removed from Goffman's initial formulations. The interaction order is *an effect* of the dialectics between the historical body and historical space. It is the actual order of communicative conduct that ensues from enskilled bodies in a space inscribed with particular conditions for communication. It has very little existence outside of it, and the three elements of the triad now form one ethnographic object of inquiry.

The Zebra Crossing

As an illustration of the way in which space is densely packed with several different discourses, and so forms a 'semiotic aggregate', the Scollons (Scollon & Wong Scollon, 2003: 180–189) analyze a very mundane thing: crossing the street in five cities. In each of the cities, such places where pedestrians can cross are littered with signs, some for the traffic, some for the pedestrians and some for both; some directly related to the regulation of crossing the street and halting the traffic, some (e.g. shop signs) unrelated to it. Pedestrians must make sense of these multiple discourses, and such sense-making processes are part of the habitual routine practice of crossing a street. With the remarks made above in mind, we would now like to return to the example of crossing a street, focusing specifically on how the nexus triad should be seen as a historically shaped complex, organizing everyday practices. I shall focus on one particular moment, documented in Figure 2.1, and explain how we can see such a moment as a moment of social semiotics.

We see someone on a zebra crossing in what looks like a relatively busy shopping street. The person (incidentally: this author) moves forward on the zebra crossing; he looks to the left and his left hand is raised in a gesture signalling 'stop', 'careful' or 'thanks'. We notice also that a bus has just passed the zebra crossing, and from Blommaert's gesture we can infer that another vehicle is approaching the zebra crossing.

The zebra crossing is on the corner of the street in Antwerp, Belgium, where Blommaert lives, and it has a history. It was only recently put there by the municipality after protracted campaigning by the neighborhood. As mentioned earlier, this is a shopping street with rather dense traffic; there is a primary school in the street, and every day hundreds of children had to cross this street without the protection of a zebra crossing. It used to be a hazardous place to cross the street and the zebra crossing significantly improved traffic safety for pedestrians. In the terminology of the Scollons, the zebra crossing would be a 'municipal regulatory discourse' (Scollon & Wong Scollon, 2003: 181–185); the fact is that the sheer existence of this zebra crossing makes a huge semiotic difference, one that is inscribed in Blommaert's gesture while crossing the street. How?

The zebra crossing flags a particular set of rights and obligations in that particular place; it creates, so to speak, a historical micro-space with a particular order. A pedestrian on a zebra crossing has right of way, and it is

Figure 2.1 To cross a street

mandatory for cars and other vehicles to halt in front of the zebra crossing. If a pedestrian crosses the street elsewhere, where there is no zebra crossing, s/he has no such rights and car drivers have no such obligations. Consequently, while car drivers would almost always and instantly halt their car when someone crosses a zebra crossing, they may hoot, flash their headlights or even start scolding and shouting at pedestrians crossing elsewhere. The zebra crossing is thus a semiotic space, a 'discourse in place' that imposes, within the small confines of that space, a particular interaction order – one into which all possible participants have been effectively enskilled. Car drivers know immediately that they should halt in front of a zebra crossing, they will scan the road ahead for such signs and will react almost instinctively when they see a pedestrian on a zebra crossing. Pedestrians, in turn, will walk towards the zebra crossing if they intend to cross the street. They know how to recognize it and they know that they should cross the street there if they intend to do it safely. The actual crossing, then, is another instance of enskillment, in which the pedestrian first looks left and right, ensuring that no danger is ahead, then moves across while keeping eye contact with approaching cars and, if necessary, communicating with them by means of gestures. Crossing a street is an act of ordered and localized communication, in which bodies interact in an orderly fashion with regulatory signs and with other participants in that space. There are dimensions of institutionality here, as well as dimensions of a more general kind of social order: people responding and adjusting to 'normal' and orderly ways of doing things.

This moment is a nexus of practice, and we see the three elements of the aggregate interacting: there is the enskilled historical body that has been adjusted to or enskilled in the orderly use of a particular historical microspace (the zebra crossing), resulting in a particular interaction order. The interaction order emerges and becomes activated as a compelling normative frame for all participants as soon as the enskilled body engages with the historical space – as soon as Blommaert, a seasoned street-crosser, walks into a space that is institutionally defined in terms of formal rights and obligations, the zebra crossing. His engagement with that space moves his body into a zone in which certain acts of communication are mandatory, expected or desired, others transgressive. He is, for instance, expected not to unnecessarily delay the crossing; car drivers would as a rule not be overly amused if he would start doing Michael Jackson's moonwalk on a zebra crossing in a busy street such as this one; the hooting and shouting would start at once, no matter how entertaining the performance may be.

The fact is: Blommaert knows this and so do the drivers. All of them have acquired the codes valid in such micro-spaces, and all of us are capable to shift in and out of such codes when we enter and leave such spaces. The next space will impose different codes, and again we will be familiar with them. Blommaert is, for instance, familiar with the shops behind him; he knows how to behave adequately there and he can shift in and out of the interaction orders valid in them in no time. As we move through daily routines, the nexuses of practice follow each other swiftly, in a matter of seconds, often with dramatic differences between them, but rarely causing dramatic problems for those who engage in them. In fact, we all possess a tremendously complex array of such enskilled knowledge, capable of navigating us through spaces that are experienced as entirely mundane and unproblematic, while they are, in fact, extraordinarily complex. We experience this complexity only, as a rule, when we leave our familiar environments and find ourselves in places where, for instance, car drivers do *not* have the obligation (or habit) to stop in front of zebra crossings. Many a broken rib or leg testifies to that sudden experience of unexpected complexity.[1]

Mainstream notions of communicative competence, with their emphasis on formal learning and acquisition and their focus on cognition, are not sufficient to cover this vast field of flexible skills we possess and deploy in our interaction with our environments. It is to the credit of the Scollons that they understood this and offered clear and stimulating suggestions for overcoming this problem. They were particularly successful in blending the small and the big dimensions of human social practice: the ways in which each act of communication is at once exceptional and typical, that it always consists of completely new forms of patterning and organization, while it derives its communicability from sharedness and recognizability of patterns. And they understood quite clearly that the way to blend these different dimensions is by introducing historical lineages to individual practices, by suggesting that uniqueness always has a pedigree, an intertext or interdiscourse that needs to be understood in the broadest possible way – that is, in relation to the totality of features of practice, including the bodily, spatial and material ones.

Their ethnography, consequently, solves the problem of synchrony. Every aspect of the synchronically observable practice – the nexus – is historically loaded, so to speak; it drags with it its histories of use, abuse and evaluation. Thus, whenever we ethnographically investigate a synchronic social act, we have to see it as the repository of a process of genesis, development, transformation. If we see it like this, we will see it in its sociocultural fullness, because we can then begin to understand the shared, conventional aspects of it, and see it as a moment of social and cultural transmission. In that move, the Scollons focused our attention on two things we are not much used to in the field of language: on bodies as repositories of histories of experience, and on space as historically organized, ordered and patterned, thus becoming a genuine actor in semiotic processes.

Note

(1) The compelling nature of our habitual expectations of such order can be illustrated by the following anecdote. Some time ago I was in Dubrovnik, Croatia, waiting for a bus to take me back to my hotel. The bus stop was very crowded: school was out and groups of students were waiting for the same bus. When the bus arrived, a titanic life-and-death battle erupted at once between the dozens of people scrambling to get on the bus. In the mayhem of that moment, I found myself shoulder to shoulder with a lady, a tourist clearly and British in addition, for she kept whispering 'there is a queue, there is a queue'.

3   Semiotic and Spatial Scope

We have seen in the previous chapter that space offers us an opportunity to bring an intrinsic historicity to what we attempt in LLS. This topic will be taken further here, and I will consider semiotized space as a material given here, inscribed with semiotic features and working according to a mode of operation that derives from the nature of these semiotic features – at least, when we approach these features from a specific perspective, and I will discuss the work of Gunther Kress in order to develop that perspective.

Let me be more precise. The attempt in this chapter fits in an intellectual project that, in my view, ties together much of Gunther Kress' work, and can also be found, among others, in Stroud and Mpendukana (2009) and in the 'geosemiotics' developed by Scollon and Wong Scollon (2003), which I discussed at greater length in the previous chapter. This project is the construction of a genuinely materialist theory of signs: a semiotics that sees signs not as primarily mental and abstract phenomena reflected in 'real' moments of enactment, but sees signs as material forces subject to and reflective of conditions of production and patterns of distribution, and as constructive of social reality, as real social agents having real effects in social life. Kress consistently calls this a *social* semiotics (e.g. Kress, 2009), but it is good to remember that methodologically, this social semiotics is a materialist approach to signs. Such a materialism reacts, of course, against the Saussurean paradigm, in which the sign was defined as *'une entité psychique'* with two faces: the signifier and the signified (Saussure, 1960: 99). The study of signs – semiotics – could so become a study of *abstract* signs; retrieving their meaning could become a matter of digging into their *deeper* structures of meaning *systems*; and semiotics could become a highly formal enterprise (for an example, see Eco, 1979).

Much of the problem resides in the way in which 'system' is imagined here; aspects of that problem have been touched upon in the previous chapter. We must now take this discussion further.

In classical structuralist approaches, a system is necessarily timeless and contextless – it is the deeper level that generates the 'real' phenomena operating in a concrete context, the 'software', so to speak, that allows an almost infinite number of applications. Systems, or 'structures', consequently display an uneasy relationship to history: the structuralist 'synchrony' was necessarily 'achronic' because it did not claim to have any empirical existence. After all, an empirical 'synchrony' in linguistics, for example, would come down to 'the recording of all the words spoken at the same time by thousands of speaking subjects' – an enterprise that Greimas, for instance, qualifies as 'rather point-less' (Greimas, 1990: 95), and which from a structuralist viewpoint would also not be worth one's while.

'System', however, can also be imagined as a *historical* given, as something that brings historical coherence (and hence, understandability) to isolated facts by means of patterns – cultural patterns such as 'classicism', historical ones such as 'absolutism', economic ones such as 'capitalism' and so on. Foucault's work addressed and decoded such systems – regimes of power/ knowledge – and much of Bourdieu's work can be read as an analysis of the class system in France. Such historically ordered patterns define systems, they are systemic, but they are not abstract. They have a real ('synchronic' or syntagmatic) existence in a plethora of individually insignificant but observable material features, and such features make sense when they are seen in their totality. This is the core methodological point in ethnography, and incidentally, also the point Bourdieu always emphasized because it is what allows us to discover 'the logic of practice' (see e.g. Bourdieu, 1990). It is such a historical, material, real system that we must keep it in mind, and the way we approach such a system is by means of ethnography.

LLS offer us a good take-off position, and the work we need to do is again relatively simple. Empirical reflections on signs in public space push us to a simple point, that signs rarely have a *general* meaning and mostly have a *specific* meaning. This pedestrian observation, however, has consequences not often realized. It draws semiotics into a different theoretical realm and propels us towards materialist and ethnographic approaches to signs. Before we get there, a few general remarks are in order.

Signs in Public

Public signs both reflect and regulate the structure of the space in which they operate. Sociological, cultural, sociolinguistic and political features of that space will determine how signs look and work in that space, and signs will contribute to the organization and regulation of that space by defining addressees and selecting audiences, and by imposing particular restrictions, offering invitations, articulating norms of conduct and so on to these selected audiences. Messages in the public space are never neutral, they always display connections to social structure, power and hierarchies (see Stroud & Mpendukana, 2009; Coupland & Garrett, 2010). The reason for this is that public space itself is an area (and instrument) of regulation and control, of surveillance and power. To go by Michel Foucault's words, 'spatial anchoring is an economic-political form that demands detailed study' (Foucault, 2001: 195, see also, Lefebvre, 2000).[1] The public space of a market square or a highway is, in contrast to the private space of, for example one's dining room, a shared space over which multiple people and groups will try to acquire authority and control, if not over the whole of the space, then at least over parts of it. It is an institutional object, regulated (and usually 'owned') by official authorities whose role will very often be clearest in the restrictions they impose on the use of space (prohibitions on smoking, loitering, littering, or speed limits, warnings and so on). Communication in the public space, consequently, is communication in a field of power; sociolinguistically, the question is: how does space organize semiotic regimes of language? (cf. Blommaert et al., 2005: 198; also Stroud & Mpendukana, 2009). The question assumes that regimes can be multiple and competing, but that they nevertheless function as regimes, i.e. as ordered patterns of normative conduct and expectations, authoritative patterns of conduct to which one should orient.

Two recent branches of scholarship have taken signs in public space as their object; they have already been introduced in earlier chapters: first of course LLS, and second, Geosemiotics (henceforth GS). To start with LLS, studies on linguistic landscapes are mainly devoted to the public visibility of multilingual phenomena within bi/tri-lingual countries and cities, such as Brussels, Belgium or Montreal, Canada. An increasing amount of work focuses on highly globalized and internationalized cities, such as Beijing (Lin, 2009) or Tokyo (Backhaus, 2007). According to Backhaus (2007: 12), 'the lack of a summarising term' could be the cause that, in spite of precursors going back to the 1970s, LLS has only become a topic in sociolinguistic studies in recent years. In these more recent formulations, 'Linguistic Landscape is concerned with languages being used on signs (hence, languages in written form) in public space' (Gorter, 2006: 11; see Juffermans, 2010 for a survey and discussion). This formulation, of course, begs all sorts of substantial methodological questions.

Let us turn to one prominent example of LLS, Backhaus' (2007) study of Tokyo. Backhaus' study is overwhelmingly quantitative: it lists the languages publicly observed in areas in Tokyo, juxtaposes them and ranks them on the basis of frequency and density of distribution. Backhaus (2007: 60) pointed out that LLS cannot develop without a clear quantitative corpus, and he refers critically to GS in this respect.

Backhaus, however, fails to spot the fundamental differences between GS and his version of LLS: the fact that according to GS, a better comprehension of the socio-cultural meaning of language material requires ethnographic understanding rather than numbers, and that signs are necessarily addressed as *multimodal* objects rather than as linguistic ones. Backhaus' study was focusing on numbers and on general linguistic description around the numbers – concretely, counting the languages we can identify on public signs. Now, signs can be a lot more interesting than that. Signs in social space tell us a lot about the users of the space, how users interacts with signs, how users influence and are influenced by them; they so start telling stories about the cultural, historical, political and social backgrounds of a certain space – the 'system' in the sense outlined earlier.

Quantitative LLS, as the very first step, will draw attention to the existence and presence of languages in a particular space and can answer questions such as 'how many languages are used in space X'? But the argument does not cut very deep, and what we get is a rather superficial, 'horizontal' and distributional image of multilingualism. The fact that these languages are ingredients of multimodal signs, and that these signs occur in non-random ways in public space, is left aside, and this is where we need to begin our own search. We can draw on some crucial insights from the work of Kress and on some fundamental notions from GS to help us in our search, so let us look at some images.

Scope and Demarcation

We will start with a (at first glance) hardly spectacular picture from London Chinatown: Figure 3.1 (below) (Huang, 2010).

This is of course a mundane sign: a no-go sign at the entrance of a parking garage in London Chinatown. We see 'text' (the Chinese writing, saying 'entrance prohibited'), as well as a conventionalized iconographic shape, the meaning of which is universally construed as 'no entrance'. Text co-occurs here with the visual shape of the sign, and from this co-occurrence we can infer that one has to do with the other: the text supports, emphasises or repeats the information contained in the non-textual, visual sign and vice versa. What will primarily interest us here is their co-occurrence and the way in which such co-occurrences actually function. Let us run through some issues that emerge at this point.

(1) Even if words, colors and shapes co-occur and interact here, the different elements still appear to operate in different ways. Kress and van Leeuwen

Figure 3.1 'No Go' sign in London Chinatown (courtesy April Huang)

(1996), as we know, defined such co-occurrences as multimodal signs and showed that the different 'modalities' (words versus shapes, colors, etc.) have different 'affordances'. One can do different things with different modalities, and constructing a multimodal sign often revolves around combining the affordances of the different modalities. Thus, while the visual shape of the sign is quite generally understood (the sign can be found all over the world, with the same meaning), the Chinese text underneath it is not understandable for all. People who do not know Chinese will not understand what the text says (even if the co-occurrence with the sign may offer plausible hypotheses about the meaning of the text). Thus, the different modalities appear to have a different *semiotic scope*: they both reach (and select) different audiences. While everyone is the addressee of the visual sign, not everyone is an addressee for the Chinese text.

(2)   The sign is also put in a specific location (the entrance to the parking lot), and the meaning of the sign is specific to that physical location (the 'no-go' message only applies to the parking lot). Scollon and Wong Scollon (2003) provide the term 'emplacement' for this: signs are placed in a *specific* space, a *non-random* place and their emplacement defines their effects. A non-smoking sign inside a pub means that smoking is prohibited *inside*, not *outside* the pub. When someone smokes inside the pub, s/he is violating a rule; when s/he smokes outside the pub, no such rule is valid there. Signs, consequently, not only have a semiotic scope (as in point (1) above), but also a *spatial scope*: they operate in particular, identified spaces, and define such spaces.

(3)   If we combine semiotic scope and spatial scope, we understand that one of the major functions of public signs is *demarcation*. Signs cut up a larger space into smaller ones, into micro-spaces where particular rules and codes operate in relation to specific audiences. As we saw in the example here, there can be overlap and conflict. In the 'no entrance' sign, we saw on the one hand an almost universal semiotic scope (that of the visual road sign) combined with a much narrower one, articulated through the Chinese writing. Both forms of demarcation cooperated with a third one, spatial scope, which restricted the effect of the sign to a particular micro-space (the entrance to the car park). But this is where we see that public signs are cultural as well as social (and even political) objects. The different modalities that enter into the signs and make it into its multi-modal outcome need to be seen in these terms: as affordances that have a cultural, social and political dimension.

(4)   They also have a *historical* dimension, and we must recall what we argued in the previous chapter. There are expectations – normative expectations – about relationships between signs and particular spaces. It is the connection between space and normativity that makes space historical.

(5)   Closely connected to this is the notion of *visual repertoire*. We all perceive and interpret signs on the basis of skills and competences we have gathered in life – the enskillment processes discussed in the previous

chapters. Such skills and competences revolve, as we have seen, around the capacity to decode and act on the explicit and implicit codes used and deployed in signs. They strongly depend, consequently, on one's social position in a particular space. Someone belonging to the established diaspora in London Chinatown (with, e.g. origins in Hong Kong) may be able to read most of the public signs that are visible there, since s/he can read (at least some forms of) Chinese script as well as Latin script. Someone entering Chinatown with an Eastern-European background, in contrast, and literacy competences restricted to the Cyrillic alphabet, will not be able to make much sense of most of the signs there, with the exception perhaps of 'universal' aspects of signs, such as the road sign in our example. The visual repertoires of both people are strongly different; the way in which they engage with and can operate in relation to signs is thus very different as well. In superdiverse spaces, such differences between visual repertoires account for much of what goes on in the way of understanding and misunderstanding.

Let us, with these remarks in mind, now turn to another image, taken from Berchem (Figure 3.2).

This handwritten sign was posted in the window of what used to be a florist shop. The shop ceased its activities a while ago, and no discernible activities were taking place in the premises until this sign appeared. The sign is written in a mixture of traditional and simplified Chinese script, and it announces: 'apartment to let: first class furnishing, water and electricity included, 350 Yuan per month' (followed by a phone number).

If we take the points made earlier and apply them here, we can see the following. The spatial scope is relatively clear: this sign operates within the space of the former shop; we can assume that activities connected to the sign would also be connected to this particular place: either the apartment is in this building, or the ones who rent it out live there.

The semiotic scope is rather clear too, even if certain questions arise here. Let me first provide an elementary semiotic principle. Every sign tells a story about who produced it, and about who is selected to consume it. In that sense (and in addition to its synchronic and syntagmatic emplacement, i.e. its 'pointing sideways'), every sign points backwards to its origins, and forward to its uptake. In more technical jargon, this is called the 'double arrow of indexicality', the fact that every sign *presupposes* things and *entails* things when it is used (Silverstein, 2006). We select it because of the presuppositions it conventionally carries, and addressees understand it on the basis of the entailments it triggers. It is at once a repository of past meanings and a vehicle for future meanings. Every sign is historical as well as proleptic.

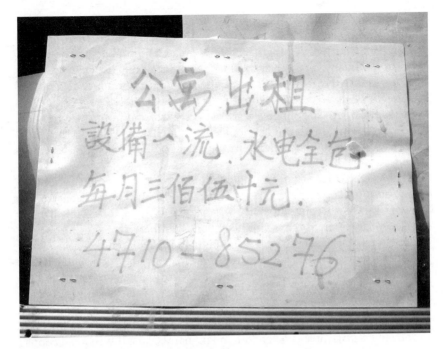

Figure 3.2 Handwritten Chinese in Berchem

This is not rocket science, but the impact of this simple semiotic statement is quite significant. If we broaden the statement somewhat, we see that a sign always contains three analytical dimensions: one towards its past, another one towards its future. The third one, in between both – we have seen this just now – is the present, characterized by the sign's non-random emplacement.

Let us now turn back to the sign in Figure 3.2. It is obvious that this sign selects 'Chinese' audiences and organizes an interaction between 'Chinese' interlocutors. The ones who rent out the apartment are in all likelihood 'Chinese' immigrants, and the people to whom they intend to let the apartment are 'Chinese' as well. The scare quotes around 'Chinese', however, suggest that this notion is far from simple here, and now we need to move into the past of the sign.

We saw that the sign is written in a mixture of traditional Mandarin script (used in, e.g. Taiwan, Hong Kong and most of the traditional Chinese diaspora), and simplified script (used in the People's Republic). The mixture suggests 'incomplete' or emergent competence in either scripts: either the author is familiar with traditional script but does his best to accommodate potential customers from the People's Republic (the largest contingent of Chinese immigrants nowadays), or vice versa. (The fact that 'Yuan' are used as identifying currency, rather than 'Euro', may lend support to the former hypothesis.) In any event, the mixed orthographic resources deployed in this sign suggest a heterogeneous, unstable and transient community of 'Chinese' in inner-city Antwerp. An attempt to describe the semiotic scope of this sign leads us, thus, into sociolinguistic aspects of signs, and from there to wider socio-political and historical developments often hardly visible to the casual observer, or even to people living in the neighborhood where this sign was placed.

The neighborhood is in fact predominantly Turkish and Belgian, as we know, both groups being the most visible (and audible) ones there. We also know that it has become superdiverse since the 1990s. Chinese immigrants have been largely invisible in this neighborhood; there are two Chinese – or to be more precise, Cantonese – restaurants that have been there since long; no other Chinese shops (e.g. groceries) have recently been opened, Chinese people are not part of the regular 'street-scape' of the neighborhood and the local schools do not count significant numbers of learners of Chinese origins. Oud-Berchem is not a Chinatown. The handwritten sign in Figure 3.2 is, in actual fact, the first piece of handwritten Chinese text I have ever observed in the public space of this neighborhood in many years. If we would adopt a quantitative linguistic landscape approach to it, it would not be a significant item; it would fall within the 'error margin' of statistical research.

But we know that the statistically insignificant can be a sign of momentous change, so let us take this one-off sign seriously. The sign demarcates a space: a very small space, just one flat. But by doing that, it adds one more claim to ownership and legitimate presence and belonging to the semiotic landscape of the neighborhood, because here is a Chinese actor interacting with other potential Chinese actors – here is, in other words, the suggestion, the possibility of an existing social network and/or the presence of an emerging community. This network, as we saw, is largely invisible when we deploy everyday forms of observation; it is also statistically insignificant; but the presence of this sign suggests a process of transition in which a hitherto invisible community enters the public space and communicates there. The public space is now theirs too, they are also recognizable in the superdiverse neighborhood where they live. The Chinese interlocutors have carved out a small space for themselves, a place they own and have exclusive access to.

The insight that signs demarcate space enables us now to make a qualitative statement about the public space. Obviously, when we compare the two signs in Figures 3.1 and 3.2, we see that the term 'public' means different things in both cases. The semiotic scope of the road sign is wider than that of the 'apartment for rent' sign, and is, in that sense more public – it addresses more potential interlocutors and excludes less. Or at least: the visual sign has a very broad scope, while the Chinese text underneath has a much narrower scope and targets a much smaller potential audience.

Public space is therefore manifestly layered and segmented; that is: space is not just a horizontal, distributional given, but also a *vertical*, stratified one. It is never uniform because the signs in public space demarcate areas and audiences, some of which are vast while others are microscopic. Road signs, for instance, would typically have a vast scope; but note that even such 'universal' signs have restrictions in spatial and semiotic scope. A sign announcing a speed limit of 70 km/hour normally has no relevance for pedestrians and, thus, does not select pedestrians as their addressees. A scribbled note posted on a door saying 'John, I'll be back in five minutes' would represent the other extreme of the scale: a very 'private' notice in public space addressing just one specific interlocutor and excluding all others.

Such different signs coexist in public space, and we must realize that they do very different things in that space. It is important to realize this, because when we encounter a forest of signs, such as in London Chinatown or in superdiverse Berchem, we can then now understand that this abundance of signs does not reflect a chaotic, disordered pattern, but reflects a form of complex order that begs investigation. Even if signs criss-cross, overlap and contradict each other, this does not mean that we are facing what may seem a random display of semiotic resources. We may be facing different interacting (and sometimes conflicting) social orders, as when different groups compete over rights of ownership of a place and contest or overwrite each other's signs (a frequent feature of graffiti). We can also be facing historical layering of signs, where older signs have become amended or erased by newer ones. In any event, the wide variety of signs raises questions about social order, agency and social structure, because each of the signs will have a particular scope and operate within that scope. Within that scope, signs have a form of agency: they order, request, ask, demand or inform people within that spatial zone. Emplacement, the central notion of GS, makes space into an active, agentive force in social life, and it points the way towards complexity in spaces such as the ones I discussed here.

I can add another qualitative statement at this point. The demarcating effect of signs in public space also defines *identities*. When potential addressees are being selected by a sign – for example, the 'apartment for rent' sign – they become something: they become potential legitimate users of the demarcated space. 'In this demarcated space, Chinese people will be legitimate users' would be the categorizing message contained in the signs mentioned here.

Such categorizations of legitimate usage, naturally, are social and political categories; they fuel the dynamics of power in public space and they are core ingredients of social and political conflicts – as when the police act against groups of young immigrant men who congregate in empty shopping malls after closing time. The shopping mall is made for 'shoppers' between 8am and 6pm; as long as one displays shopping behavior there and then, one is a legitimate user of that space. After 6pm, however, it can become a skaters' paradise or a haven for homeless people seeking shelter for the night. Ownership and legitimate use of such spaces change during the course of the day, and conflicts often ensue from denials of, or contests about, such changes – as when the shopping mall management refuse to turn their space over to skaters and homeless people after 6pm and send in the police to remove them from the grounds.

The upshot of this, however, is that when we walk through a street, *our identities can and do change every few steps* – from someone who is included in a communication network, to someone who is excluded from it and back; and through this, from someone who belongs to a particular network or community, to someone who does not belong, and back. We do not consciously feel such immediate changes in identity because we do not choose them. The signs select them for us and pin them upon us – space is, in that sense, agentive. We may experience these identities, though, when we feel 'out of place', when we enter a shop or a bar in which we are not members of the 'normal' community of users. It is when people stare at us upon entering, or when we find that the people in that space are amazed, scared, disturbed or irritated by our presence there, that we realize that space has done something to us.

We can also make the notion of 'transgression' somewhat more specific now. Signs emplaced outside of their legitimate space – graffiti would be a typical instance – violate the rules of demarcation that apply to specific areas. Thus, a piece of a graffiti on, say, a monument for war heroes, can quickly be seen as an 'insult', an expression of a 'lack of respect' – respect for what? For the rules of legitimate use of that space, which is strictly regulated, and grossly violated by the intrusive acts of graffiti artists. Similar judgments apply to graffiti painted on someone's house: such graffiti is seen as a violation of the property rights of the house owners. The owner of the house is typically the one – the only one – who can decide on its looks, decoration and so forth. It is strictly *the owner's space*, and only the owner has control over the spatial and semiotic scope of his/her property. Transgressive signs, thus, violate the demarcating power of rules of legitimate access and usage of space.

Thus, many, if not most, real spaces operate on a 'members only' basis. And this, of course, is a *systemic* observation.

High-Octane LLS

The central insight I developed in this chapter is, as said at the outset, fundamentally trivial. It is the fact that most signs have a specific meaning, not a general one. The meaning and effect of signs, in actual social life, is not unlimited or unrestricted; it is specific to the space in which they are emplaced and to the addressees they select.

This trivial insight brings us into a different realm of analysis, though. We cannot be satisfied by stating that the sign in Figure 3.1 means 'no entrance' *in general*. It is a real sign planted non-randomly in a real space, and it has a precise function there chosen by deliberate human action. It transforms that space into a social and political object, an object of control, surveillance, power. Why? Because it is not just *a* sign, an unspecified sign, but because it is *this particular* sign, a sign planted at the entrance of a parking garage in London Chinatown.

A social, or a materialist, semiotics starts from this fact: that this is not just any sign, but a specific one, and that we can only understand it when we dissect the specifics of its appearance and function. This social or materialist semiotics, thus, adopts an ethnographic point of departure: that social and cultural phenomena are situated, and that to understand them means that we have to understand their situatedness. Other exercises are, to adopt Greimas' words again, rather pointless.

We arrive at an entirely different LLS when we see signs in public space as multimodal signs situated in a concrete and non-random context. In addition, it is through concentrated attention to semiotization – concretely, attention to multimodal signs – that we can turn space into a genuinely ethnographic object, full of traces of human activity, interactions, relations, histories and anticipated futures. We have turned LLS from a rather complex tool for performing a very basic operation – counting languages – into a simple tool for performing analyses of complexity. From a 'light' LLS, we now have a high-octane variety, and an entirely new story of social and historical analysis can begin from there. I suggest we take these ideas and insights and deploy them in the neighborhood I introduced earlier: Oud-Berchem. The next chapters will be devoted to that.

Note

(1) The French original reads: «L'ancrage spatial est une forme économico-politique qu'il faut étudier en detail».

4 Signs, Practices, People

The theoretical remarks made in the two previous chapters have made clear that (1) semiotized space is not neutral, but replete with codes, norms, criteria for inclusion and exclusion, membership categories and identities. (2) Using space involves learning these codes, norms and criteria – enskillment – and acting habitually in relation to them. Whenever we use space, we orient towards the messages we pick up in such spaces and we act accordingly. We identify a space as a no-go area, and area where someone like us is not welcome, and we avoid entering it. Recognizing the codes, norms and criteria of semiotized spaces is part of the vast array of knowledge that we often label as 'social skills' or as 'cultural competences'. Being enskilled in them, and consequently being capable of acting by orienting towards them, is probably a good definition of 'integration'.

I came to these theoretical remarks by casting an ethnographic gaze onto linguistic landscaping. This is an epistemological as well methodological move, in which I addressed space as an arena of human social and cultural action, and in which space can be 'read' in relation to such forms of action because space is a complex and layered repository of traces of such action. There is no language without communication patterns in which that language is involved; more in general, there are no signs without communication patterns. By looking at public signs, therefore, we can perform *a reconstruction of the communication patterns for which such signs were manufactured.* Communication patterns are, in turn, social patterns, and an ethnographic study of situated signs can thus lead us towards insights into the social structure in which they fit. Signs lead us to practices, and practices lead us to people: individuals and groups who live in a given area in a particular configuration, with a particular degree of regulation and order, and with different forms of social and cultural organization in relation to each other. This sequence, from signs to practices to people, is the true analytic potential of linguistic landscaping.

I will now take the theoretical instruments developed so far and apply them to an area I am very familiar with and of which we have already seen glimpses in the previous chapters: the neighborhood Oud-Berchem in Antwerp, Belgium, my own home. In what follows I will try to provide a more consistent and coherent description of this area.

As we shall see, this neighborhood is superdiverse, and for several years now I have been collecting data on developments and transformations in the neighborhood, using linguistic landscaping as the main instrument for what now amounts to longitudinal ethnographic fieldwork. This longitudinal aspect raises a set of methodological issues, connected to an earlier issue. In the previous chapters I emphasized the historical dimension of space – the fact that semiotization historicizes space, in such a way that every sign points backwards towards the conditions of production of the sign and forward to its potential uptake. Every sign is a trace of situated actions in the past and a template of future actions.

To this historization we can now add another dimension. Linguistic landscaping has so far largely confined itself to a 'snapshot' approach – the synchrony of traditional sociolinguistic and ethnographic research. I will argue, *contra* this position, that linguistic landscaping is an extraordinary tool for *historical* ethnographic research. By means of linguistic landscaping, we can follow in great detail the changes and transformations of the social order we can distinguish through the complex semiotic organization of space.

This invites fundamental theoretical reflections, which I shall develop in more detail in the final chapter of this study; but let me say this. In combination with the first issue – the sign as a historical trace of social action – the diachronic deployment of linguistic landscaping offers a rather definitive argument against linguistic landscaping as a synchronic analytical tool. Linguistic landscaping can be all kinds of things, but not an a-historical inquiry; it is an instrument for historical research. This research – 'reading back' from signs to practices and people – is of great relevance for the study of the superdiverse forms of social order characterizing our contemporary societies.

I have introduced the neighborhood in Chapter 1. Linguistic landscaping can help us in dissecting its complex and delicate structures. I will ask and discuss three questions: (1) who lives there? (2) Do we see forms of organization? And if so, how? (3) Do we see traces of change and transformation? The latter question will be addressed in the next chapter. What follows is, thus, an attempt to use ethnographic linguistic landscaping in an attempt to arrive at a detailed and accurate *synchronic* description of the neighborhood, oriented towards questions of demographic and social presence in the area.

Who Lives Here?

Let us begin where most of linguistic landscaping begins: by counting languages. For several years I have been doing a two- to three-weekly walk through the Statiestraat–Driekoningenstraat, counting the publicly visible languages. I never counted less than 11, and a maximum of 24 languages. A comprehensive list of the languages displayed in the Statiestraat–Driekoningenstraat over the several years I observed them would be this:

- Dutch
- French
- English
- Turkish
- Arabic
- Russian
- Polish
- Mandarin Chinese
- Cantonese
- Thai
- Farsi
- Spanish
- Portuguese
- Tamil
- Hindi
- Urdu
- Albanian
- Serbo-Croatian
- Italian
- German
- Armenian
- Bulgarian
- Japanese
- Latin

All these languages appeared on inscriptions in the street, and all of them were publicly visible from the sidewalk – I did not go and look at messages next to door bells and other more private inscriptions. But that is where the level of general observation stops. The inscriptions are of a wide variety of types, and the languages occur in greatly differing levels of density and patterns of distribution. So let me be more specific.

Types of signs

We first need to look at the different types of signs, and follow common sense here. Distinctions of signs into various types – a first amendment to a horizontal and distributional bias in linguistic landscaping – have started to be made (see Coupland & Garrett, 2010; Jaworski, 2010), and they are fundamental for understanding the social dynamics behind the inscriptions. But rather than to try and force my data into existing typologies, I opt for a simple and superficially descriptive, but immediately helpful, categorization. We see three broad categories of signs.

(a) *Permanent signs*: road signs, shop signs, permanent publicity signs, landmarks, graffiti.
(b) *Event-related signs*: posters; temporary shop signs (announcing, e.g. discounts or particular products); for-rent or for-sale signs; smaller announcements displayed publicly (e.g. announcing absence, change of address, etc.).
(c) *'Noise'*: inscriptions that landed in the neighborhood 'by accident': people leaving readable objects behind; cars and vans stationed for a brief while. These objects are in the landscape, but not as an effect of deliberate landscaping.[1]

While categories (a) and (b) point towards sedentary producers – people permanently residing in the neighborhood – and to different kinds of activities performed by such people, category (c) can be helpful in identifying 'passers by', people drifting in and out of the neighborhood, semipermanent residents, visitors and so forth. The different types of inscriptions thus already raise questions about social structure and social dynamics.

We must go further though, and delve into the connections between inscriptions and activities. Let me disregard for the moment the road signs; their highly specific character has been mentioned earlier and they do not particularly inform us on the social structure of the neighborhood. Focusing on the other signs, we see differences as well.

(a) Some signs have *landmark* functions, i.e. functions that identify a particular area in relation to history, tradition and customs. In this neighborhood, there is one such sign: a stone pillar with a statue of Mary on top, and with the Latin inscription 'Mater Dei Sine Peccata in Conceptione' ('Mother of God without sin in conception'). This is the only instance of Latin in the neighborhood; the language does not point towards a particular community of language users, but points to a

ritual, religious tradition. The sign selects everyone as its potential audience; the use of Latin, however, excludes virtually everyone as an effective 'linguistic' audience – an audience that can *read* the sign – and
reduces them to an 'indexical' audience – an audience that can pick up
the indirect meanings provided by the sign by its emplacement and
construction.

(b)   Other signs have *recruitment* functions: they invite particular groups of
people into interaction with their producers. Shop signs are the most conspicuous type here: they announce (a) the kind of transactions performed
in that place (selling vegetables versus performing financial services); (b)
the kinds of audiences targeted for such transactions. Event-related posters also belong to this category. The use of languages is critical in this
regard, and I shall return to this issue in great detail below.

(c)   Still other signs *inform* potential audiences in more detail about the activities performed in certain places. Discount announcements, rates advertised, notices announcing a change of address or temporary absence also
fall into this category. This category is *subordinate* to the previous one.
The recruitment signs would inform someone, e.g. that this is an internet café; informing signs then, in a second stage, communicate the rates
of phone calls and internet use.

(d)   Another category of signs has the function of *public statement*. Graffiti
would be the most immediately identifiable type in this category. In
contrast with most of the signs in the previous categories, public statements such as graffiti cannot be easily traced to a specific producer (a
shop owner, an identified organization), but are manufactured by producers who remain unknown and unidentifiable (except for a small in-
crowd in the case of graffiti tags). The addressee, however, can be quite
identifiable, and language choice as well as features of graphic shape
contribute to this; the same features enable us to make informed guesses
about the producer as well. Thus, a Dutch-language graffiti reading
'Belgen Pedo's' ('Belgians pedophiles') is in all likelihood produced by
someone who does not self-identify as 'Belgian', and the choice of Dutch
reveals that the selected audience are the local 'Belgians' in the area.

(e)   Finally, there is a category of *muted* signs, signs that are only indirectly
functioning as readable signs. A plastic bag containing rubbish is primarily a rubbish bag; the inscriptions on the bag are only indirectly an
instrument for communication. The bag was not initially intended as a
sign-to-be-read by others, a sign made in order to involve other people
into a specific kind of interaction. Many of the 'accidental' signs in our
earlier categorization would fall into this category: potential signs left
in the landscape without being an effect of intentional sign making.

Such rather obvious distinctions between signs are vital for any analysis we can contemplate here. It is on the basis of such distinctions that we see that the 24 languages listed above can be subdivided into several important categories – as languages *that perform specific functions* through various types of signs. It is by introducing *qualitative* distinctions between signs that we can make the move from counting languages to understanding how they can inform us about social structure. So let us now take a closer look at the 24 languages we counted in the Statiestraat–Driekoningenstraat.

Sociolinguistic stratification

The languages that are publicly displayed in the Statiestraat–Driekoningenstraat are not equal; there are clear distinctions of 'rank' and prominence, and they partly overlap with the history of habitation in the area.

(1) The language that dominates both in terms of historical continuity and in the relationship with other languages is *Dutch*. Obviously, Dutch is both the 'substrate' language – the language of the people who historically were the most numerous and enduring in terms of demography – and the official language of the area. Consequently, official signs, such as road signs, directions and official regulatory signs (e.g. building permit announcements, signs indicating the maximum number of people allowed in a public space), are all in Dutch and would be monolingual. And owing to the historical dominance of Dutch-speaking habitation, old shop signs as well as new signs targeting a wide and undifferentiated audience would be Dutch. Consider Figure 4.1.

We see two shops here; the one on the right is a photographer's shop specializing in photo cameras and mobile phones. The shop has been owned by the same local family for two generations now, and Dutch is the language of most signs there. The shop on the left is a more recently opened butchery owned by a man of Moroccan descent. The shop signs are in immaculate Dutch, even if the meat sold there is entirely halal, and even if the one exception is a calligraphic Arabic sign with the name of Allah displayed inside the shop.

Figure 4.1 also suggests another aspect of Dutch in this neighborhood: Dutch is the *spoken* lingua franca among the highly diverse populations there. When a Polish construction worker visits a Turkish-owned Do It Yourself shop, a highly truncated variety of Dutch would be the medium of communication. In public signs, this lingua franca function of Dutch can be seen from the density with which it appears in multilingual signage. No other language would be used as frequently as Dutch

Figure 4.1 Dutch prominence

in multilingual signs; combined with the previous aspects – historic-demographic prominence and official status – this lingua franca function renders Dutch into the most visible and audible language in the neighborhood. Various aspects of this dominance are combined in Figure 4.2: the shop window of a now vacant Polish-owned hair saloon with equivalent Polish and Dutch signs, which also carries an official 'for rent' sign in Dutch.

Later on, I shall dig deeper into the many shapes of Dutch in this neighborhood, and we shall see that there is not just stratification *between* languages, but also *within* languages. But for the moment, let us concentrate on the former.

(2) *Turkish* would be the second most prominent language in the neighborhood, and this of course reflects the history of Turkish presence there as well. Most Turkish inscriptions would be part of *bilingual* signs, along with Dutch. Turkish words and phrases would include the name of the shop and of some products (e.g. food items, such as börek or durum, see Figure 4.3). Monolingual Turkish signs would be restricted to posters announcing events in the Turkish community.

(3) The lower number of people of Moroccan origin in the neighborhood does not mean that they are absent, and *Arabic* would consequently be

Figure 4.2 Polish–Dutch bilingualism

a visible language as well. As with Turkish, most Arabic messages would occur in a bilingual organization along with Dutch, and monolingual Arabic signs would be restricted to posters and other announcements, and to religious inscriptions.

(4) *Polish* has over the past handful of years rapidly emerged as a visible language in the neighborhood. The hair salon in Figure 4.2 already testified to that, although it must be said that Polish-owned businesses are rare: apart from the hair salon, a Polish Delikatessen store was opened quite recently. Polish, however, mostly appears in multilingual contexts along with several other languages – English, Russian, Arabic and Dutch. Polish would typically be a *subordinate* language, an add-on to other languages, targeting one specific audience: the dozens of male Polish construction workers who reside in the neighborhood. We can see this clearly in Figure 4.4, where people from the Indian subcontinent operating an internet café annex night shop, and using English as their main language of signage, have added two small Polish signs to their window.

(5) This brings us to the second major lingua franca in the neighborhood: *English*. Internet cafés, night shops and some groceries use English as their major language of signage; very often, these shops would be operated by people of Asian and African descent, and quite often, English

Figure 4.3 Turkish–Dutch bilingualism

would be surrounded by a range of other languages: we already noted Polish, other languages include Tamil, Hindi, Urdu, Farsi and Thai. Of particular interest is the use of English in some of the recently opened Pentecostal churches in the neighborhood: I will devote Chapter 6 specifically to these religious places. And finally, English is often also the language of graffiti and publicity posters in the neighborhood, as can

Figure 4.4 Polskie Piwo

be seen in Figure 4.5. Note, in passing, the nonnative character of the English in Figure 4.5 ('send' should be 'sent').

(6) *Spanish* and *Portuguese* have over the past handful of years emerged as very visible languages, and they are strongly connected with new Pentecostal churches in the neighborhood. Prior to their arrival, publicly visible Spanish was confined to one bakery in the area.

(7) The most visible languages have now been listed. Other languages would be rare and highly specific to certain places. *Cantonese* is the language of the two Chinese restaurants in the Statiestraat; *Bulgarian* is used in one recently opened grocery; *Tamil* can be found on event-related posters displayed in a couple of shops owned by people from Southern India and Sri Lanka; *Hindi* in posters announcing Bollywood movies for sale in the same shops; *Farsi* is used (alongside Russian, English and Dutch) in one night shop operated by a couple from Afghanistan; *Albanian* was recorded once on a poster announcing the performance of an Albanian musician; *Mandarin Chinese* was confined to the handwritten sign we mentioned in the previous chapter (Figure 3.2). And so on: languages appear as if out of the blue, remain visible for a while and then disappear again. Or they are part of the more permanent linguistic landscape of the area, but confined to one or a small number of places.

Figure 4.5 English publicity

(8)   For outsiders vaguely familiar with Belgium, an obvious question might be: what about *French*? French is very rare in this neighborhood. It can be found in the names of Moroccan-owned shops ('croissanterie'), but apart from that, it is conspicuous in its absence. When it appears, it is interesting precisely because of its minimal presence in the area, and I will discuss a case below.

(9)   Note, finally, that the visible languages do not overlap entirely with the ethnolinguistic composition of the area. In fact, they probably represent only *part* of the languages actually in use in the neighborhood. We do not see, for instance, any written African languages, while significant numbers of West- and Central-African people frequent the churches, which I shall discuss in Chapter 6. Large numbers of languages are hidden by lingua francae, such as English and Arabic, and whenever we see these lingua francae, we must understand them as such: as useful languages that enable an ethnolinguistically diverse group to communicate.

In sum, languages occur in the neighborhood not as juxtaposed and equivalent items, but in a clear and transparent stratification, in which Dutch is unchallenged as the leading language, followed by Turkish, which appears most often in a bilingual pattern along with Dutch. Arabic and

Polish follow at some distance; English defines specific places and activities, and Spanish and Portuguese are entirely connected to religious practices in the neighborhood. Other languages in the neighborhood appear not to have a stable presence there, and even if they do (as with Cantonese – the Chinese restaurants have been there for many years), their low frequency does not really define the linguistic landscape of the area.

Forms of Organization

The layering and stratification of languages and signs reflects different forms of ownership and different patterns of organization, ranging from the almost-permanent and fully developed social and cultural organization attached to Dutch and, to a lesser extent, Turkish, to the highly volatile and ephemeral presence of passers-by and occasional visitors to the neighborhood. Several clues can be used in searching for such different forms of organization.

(a) The public presence and visibility of signs not only suggest the presence of both producers and potential audiences in the neighborhood, but also forms of *legitimacy* of presence and of activities. They thus also signify *voice*. To start with the presence of producers and audiences: when someone sticks up an Albanian poster on a shop window, we can plausibly infer that there are Albanian people in the neighborhood responsible for the display of the poster; and we can plausibly infer that this poster is aimed at Albanians who might read it. This is again not rocket science, but it is a step we cannot skip in our analysis.

(b) As to legitimacy: shop front signs, as a rule, are meant to recruit, attract and inform, not to provoke or scare people. It is not unusual to find flyers and smaller posters *inside* shops announcing meetings and activities of 'members-only' associations – social, cultural, religious and political, and invariably in the languages of the organizing community. Such events can be politically sensitive and controversial. There are radical Muslims in the neighborhood who organize political meetings, but one will rarely see a publicly visible sign announcing such meetings. Information is passed on verbally or by means of small flyers. The same for Tamil activists: flyers announcing meetings and other activities can be found inside shops and are written in Tamil, but are hardly ever seen on shop windows (a Tamil shop in the neighborhood had its shop windows smashed three times in two weeks' time – a sure sign of controversy and conflict in the Tamil community in the neighborhood). Cheap flights to Mecca will be announced inside groceries and hair salons; signs appealing to Muslims to quit smoking as part of the discipline of Ramadan were visible on shop windows. People thus make distinctions between signs that can be made visible for all, and signs that are for more restricted circulation and uptake. The way signs are displayed points towards such distinctions.

(c) The *shape* of signs also tells us a lot about forms of organization. 'Amateurish' signs betray lower levels of organization than 'professional' ones, and we shall see later that clear patterns of development can be observed on the basis of this clue. Handwritten or PC-printed notices have a more volatile and 'unofficial' character than signs produced by lettering and printing shops, and are usually temporary signs or signs that point towards an emergent, inchoate form of organization. We shall see examples of such emergent organizations below. The use of languages – monolingual versus multilingual – and the 'quality' of languages naturally also informs us about forms of organization.

(d) Finally, signs that fit the broader patterns of signage in the neighborhood of course reflect a more lasting structure than signs that deviate from those patterns. Thus, we need to distinguish between *common* signs and *exceptional* ones. Concretely: if graffiti are a common feature of signage in the neighborhood, new graffiti will not be perceived as remarkable and extraordinary. Here, too, we can see development: extraordinary, exceptional signs can become a more enduring structure when they remain in place and when more of them are added. This is the case of signs pointing towards religious activities: exceptional a decade ago, they are now a common and familiar feature of signage in the neighborhood.

Let us now look at some examples. I will focus, first, on degrees of solidity in organization, readable from the 'amateurish' nature of some signs. After that, I will focus on ephemeral signs, signs that inform us about occasional, accidental or nomadic presences in the neighborhood.

Old and new organizations

As mentioned above, the particular shape and quality of signs can inform us about degrees of organization. Professionally manufactured posters are expensive commodities, and those who manufacture them must have the resources to finance the printing and must be confident that the poster will attract audiences big enough to recuperate the investment. We are talking here about communities large enough to organize events of a particular size and scope, probably also communities with a lasting presence and with a degree of socio-economic and cultural resilience. In our neighborhood, there would be three communities that satisfy these criteria: the native Dutch-speaking people, the Turkish and the Moroccan community. Each of these communities has access to a network of public and private facilities, can mobilize significant capital to organize large-scale events and has a tradition of doing so.

Figure 4.6 shows a poster announcing, in Turkish, a party with live performances held in a town about 30 kilometers away. The latter feature in

Figure 4.6 A Turkish event

itself signals a level of entrenchment: the Turkish community is present in almost every town in the country, and members of that community are networked trans-locally, between Belgian towns and between Belgium and Turkey. This network is strong (and wealthy) enough to bring a star such as Tekin Keçe from Turkey to Belgium. We see a very well organized, solid and self-confident community here, capable of organizing elevated and expensive cultural and entertainment events in their own language, targeting affluent young people from within their community.

Compare now Figure 4.7, a poster found on the shop window of a small Asian grocery. The poster is in Spanish and is issued by the 'Associacion de Ecuatorianos Residentes en Amberes', the Association of Ecuadorians living in Antwerp. The grocery is just a few meters away from a Latin-American Pentecostal church. The poster announces the start of some sports activities organized by this association in a local indoor sports hall. In contrast to the Turkish poster in 4.6, the lettering, layout and esthetics of this poster tell us that it is made with modest resources – it is an 'amateurish' poster. The Ecuadorians, also in contrast to the Turkish community, are a new community in Antwerp, and it is not unlikely that the 'Associacion' is one of the first formal organizations within that community in Antwerp – it is an emergent form of organization of this new community in the area, and we can sense the difference in the solidity of both communities from features of the signs they display in public.

We can see a similar phenomenon in Figure 4.8: a poorly printed A4 poster in Polish, issued by a recently launched Polish organization called 'Strefa'. Note the differences with the surrounding signs. The Polish poster is stuck on the outside of the window of a phone shop run by an elderly Asian man and it is flanked by fully professional commercial posters in Dutch and English from mobile phone providers, and by handmade English-language A4 posters announcing the rates for phone calls to a range of countries, also identified by their national flags. We can clearly see the differences between producers here. As for the Polish poster, it announces live performances by a Polish singer, and so typologically connects with the Turkish poster in Figure 4.6. A comparison of both posters of course reveals a lot about the level of organization behind each of them.

Like the Ecuadorians, the Polish people are a relatively new community in the neighborhood. I already mentioned that their presence there is connected to temporary activities in the construction industry. We also saw that some Polish shops have been opened and that some non-Polish night shops advertise the sale of Polish products in Polish. The little A4 poster in Figure 4.8 adds to this image of the emergent organization of a Polish community in the neighborhood. The fact that we find this poster

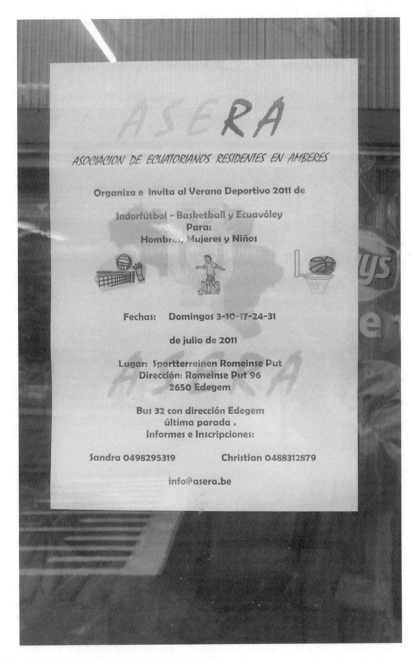

Figure 4.7 Ecuadorian emergent organizations

Figure 4.8 Polish poster in a phone shop

on the window of a phone shop is of course not a coincidence: temporary migrants such as the Polish construction workers have no official residence in the area; consequently they have no land lines or internet connection in their accommodation, as an official address is required to apply for such facilities. As an effect of this, they are intensive customers of the phone shops in the area.

Differences in the shape and quality of signs, thus, point towards differences in the ways in which communities are organized and, indirectly, in the history of presence they have in the neighborhood; and they inform us about processes of emergence and development of such communities. They also inform us circumstantially about things such as legitimacy and voice. Communities who publicly announce cultural events in their languages display some degree of confidence – the confidence that enables them to set up activities for groups of people who want or need it, and whose presence and patronage will solidify the emergent community. The fact that they advertise in their language in public spaces signals self-confidence too: they claim a legitimate presence as a community in the neighborhood – a separate community strong enough to organize itself around individuals, associations and events, and around symbols such as music, celebrities and a common language.

Accidental presence

In the little typology I offered at the beginning of this chapter, I mentioned three main types of signs: permanent signs, event-related ones and 'noise', i.e. accidental ones. We have so far considered examples of the first two types. A superdiverse neighborhood such as the one we investigate here, however, also counts numerous occasional or periodic visitors – nonresidents visiting relatives or friends, shopping or attending religious events. They too are producers and consumers of signs, and from the signs they leave we can again infer quite a bit of information about modes of organization, the nature of networks of people in the neighborhood and so forth.

Consider Figure 4.9. It is an example of that other type mentioned earlier, the 'indirectly functioning' sign. We see a rubbish bag left on a street corner. This is not an uncommon feature: official garbage bags need to be purchased at an elevated (some would say: scandalous) price, and on garbage collection days one would see a good number of ad-hoc garbage bags, mostly on street corners. Mundane objects such as plastic shopping bags are not usually considered to be reading material; yet they very often carry inscriptions – publicity – and this can tell us a thing or two.

Figure 4.9 Western Union garbage bag

The bag we see in Figure 4.9 is issued by Western Union, a low-tech money transfer provider whose presence in neighborhoods is a sure symptom of superdiversity. People who have no permanent or legal residence cannot open a bank account in Belgium. Consequently, when they need to do financial transactions, they have to rely on systems such as Western Union or Moneygram (of which we saw a poster in Figure 4.5). Several such services are present in the Statiestraat–Driekoningenstraat; Western Union itself, however, has no station in the neighborhood. The bag does not come from there; it was brought there from somewhere else.

Where from? Interestingly, the bag's imprint is in French. I already mentioned the near-absence of French as a language of public inscriptions in the neighborhood – an effect of linguistic nationalism in Flanders. The fact that the text on the bag is in French tells us that it must have been brought there from Brussels; the connection established with Goffin Change (a Belgian Exchange bureau with outlets in Brussels) confirms this. And the excellent railway connections between our neighborhood and Brussels further lend credibility to this. The bag is quite likely from Brussels.

Who brought the bag? In all likelihood, it must be someone who lives in Brussels and uses Western Union services – someone not having a permanent or legal residence in Brussels in other words. The bag is brought by a recent immigrant from Brussels, visiting the neighborhood for purposes we cannot be certain of, leaving the plastic bag there to be converted into a garbage bag.

The Synchronic Picture

What we have seen so far confirms the superdiverse nature of the neighborhood. We have seen how, in a synchronically observable space, signs testify to the presence of widely different groups and individuals engaged in a variety of activities there. Some of these groups and activities are residential, their presence is if not permanent, then at least longitudinal. Other groups are recent and their presence can be transient and temporary. Methodologically, we saw how the actual shape of signs could point towards identifying the different forms of presence and activities in the area.

Broadly generalizing, we see three different superimposed 'layers', so to speak, of populations in the area.

(1) Long-term residential communities, notably native Belgians and Turkish immigrants.
(2) Relatively stable new immigrants: Polish construction workers, African and Asian shopkeepers (groceries, internet shops, nightshops).

(3) Transient, short-term resident or newly arrived communities: Chinese, Tamil, Latin American, Eastern European.

The typology of signs and the close attention we paid to their emplacement testified to this layered demographic image: the signs we observed in their synchronic juxtaposition displayed *qualitative* differences, and such differences pointed towards difference in the nature and length of presence of different groups in the neighborhood as well as to aspects of voice and legitimacy of presence.

The next step is logical, and already announced in several statements in this chapter. We need to move from synchronic and syntagmatic description to historical analysis. The synchronic description already bumped into questions that can only be answered by looking at the historicity of signs – a purely synchronic linguistic landscaping exercise is, thus, just a first step in a more comprehensive analysis.

Note

(1) Note, however, that cars or vans can be frequently stationed in the same spot and so become an effective part of the familiar linguistic landscape of the area. I am indebted to Adam Jaworski for drawing my attention to this interesting point.

5 Change and Transformation

Let us recapitulate: a complexity paradigm necessarily historicizes its object, because in every synchronically available space we see different historicities coinciding, 'synchronized' as I called it. The survey of signs in the previous section pointed towards the simultaneous, synchronic presence of widely different groups and individuals in the same space. A closer analysis of these signs, however, can also point towards the different histories characterizing the presence of different groups in the neighborhood. Thus, if we go back to Figures 4.4 and 4.8, it is clear that the Polish signs have been superimposed – that is, added at a later stage – onto the already existing and more durable signs of the internet shops where I found them. The Polish signs are *changes* to an existing landscape, they are recent arrivals as signs, reflecting newly immigrated communities in the area – the Polish building workers are a relatively recent feature of the neighborhood. They also testify, as we saw, to emerging forms of community organization. Even though the Polish immigrants are relatively new, the group of Polish people has become a relatively stable fixture, while the actual members of the group are not always the same.

We saw the same diachronic pattern in Figures 4.6 and 4.7. A professionally manufactured Turkish poster signals a more entrenched community, confident about its legitimacy as a group in the neighborhood. The homemade poster of the Latino community, in contrast, signals a more recently immigrated community making its first strides towards community organization and consolidation in the area.

The Transformation of the Turkish Community

But there is more. Naturally, the three layers of the population I identified at the end of the previous chapter are not static, nor are they homogeneous. I have already pointed out that the area has seen, over the last handful of years, an influx of well-to-do, highly educated young native Belgians, attracted by relatively affordable real estate prices. Their immigration has considerably inflated the real estate prices, especially for the type of properties these more affluent people are looking for: relatively large middle-class houses with a garden, in which some creative restyling can be done. These affluent newcomers now live next to an older, retired native working-class population, and both groups have very different demographic and socio-economic characteristics, very different lifestyles, forms of mobility and modes of consumption, and even different political preferences, attitudes towards religion and patterns of interaction with other individuals and groups. The 'native' layer of the population in the neighborhood is, indeed, deeply divided and class-stratified.

What is more interesting, however, is the internal dynamics in the older resident immigrant community, the Turkish. Developments within this community represent a major class-stratificating process in the neighborhood.

As we know, the Turkish community have immigrated into the neighborhood in the 1970s; their presence, consequently, spans now approximately three generations. Until about a decade ago, their socio-economic characteristics were similar to those observed among other immigrant groups in many urban centers in Western Europe. Turkish immigrant communities would typically be composed of larger-than-average families with lower-than-average income. Male workers would be employed in low-skilled labor, often in vulnerable and conjuncture-sensitive sectors of the industry; chronic unemployment and underemployment would therefore be widespread. Formal employment would be supplemented by small-scale commerce, usually in groceries, bakeries or small pita and chips shops. The members of that community would typically own the houses they live in, and the value of their real estate would be very low – they would live in properties that aroused hardly any market interest.

Superdiversity has triggered a rapid process of class restratification. We have seen that new waves of immigration entered the neighborhood in the mid-1990s. Since then, we have witnessed a spectacular increase in social mobility in the Turkish community. The low-value houses they owned suddenly became a potential economic asset of sorts, as the demand for cheap accommodation in the neighborhood rose. Houses were rapidly transformed into rental accommodation with several small studios tailored to a market of short-term, transient or occasional residents. A young man called Hakan, son of a small local grocer, put in place a Do-It-Yourself business that was instantly successful and has since grown into a veritable empire with several outlets and more specialized add-ons for paint, wallpaper, windows,

Figure 5.1 Hakan Do It Yourself

plumbing and so forth (Figure 5.1). The entire neighborhood now bears the marks of rebuilding and transformation done with material from Hakan's DIY.

The influx of capital in the community created spatial mobility as well, as several Turkish families left their houses, now transformed into rental properties, and purchased properties in a more residential and middle-class suburb of Antwerp. Thus, while Turkish people still own and operate the ground-floor shops or businesses, several are no longer resident there – the demography of the neighborhood has been rather profoundly changed.

Moving from the working class to a capital-intensive business such as real estate, of course, requires more than building skills. And here, a second and slower transformation within the Turkish community enters the picture and joins forces with the rapid rise of economic opportunity in the neighborhood.

Second and third-generation Turkish immigrants increasingly obtain higher and more specialized qualifications (involving, inevitably, high levels of bilingual proficiency in Turkish and Dutch). And while gaining access to the more prestigious law firms and finance corporations may still be slow and difficult, the new economic dynamics in the neighborhood offered an opportunity for young highly educated professionals to shape a new layer of 'ethnic' enterprise: service industries. The neighborhood now counts two Turkish-owned law offices, a Turkish GP and a dentist, several financial services and accounting firms, a Turkish-owned franchise of a major bank, an industrial cleaning enterprise and a Turkish general contractor. In addition, a local branch of a major chain of pharmacies now has a Turkish female pharmacist on its staff; Turkish entrepreneurs have moved in to more specialized trades, such as advertising, lettering and printing; and some Turkish traders have managed to upscale their small groceries to the level of local supermarkets. Thus, we see a new class stratum and a repertoire of economic activity among Turkish residents, not replacing the older forms of ethnic commerce, but adding to it. Figure 5.2 illustrates this: we see a Turkish-owned pita and chips shop next to a recently opened Turkish-owned law firm.

It is thanks to the assistance of these new specialized professionals that the transformation of the neighborhood could take place; and it was the influx of new and superdiverse groups of immigrants into the neighborhood – a new and cheap labor force – that provoked the economic opportunity for new forms of business to set up camp and do quite well in the neighborhood.

Figure 5.2 Turkish law firm (left) next to Turkish pita and chips shop (right)

Thus, two kinds of historicity merge here in one process: the *durée* of gradual upward mobility across generations in the Turkish community coincides with a shorter-term historical fact, the changing nature of immigration into the neighborhood. And these two coinciding processes shaped one new dynamic of change – the rapidly evolving new entrepreneurial elite among the Turkish immigrants, driven by real-estate activities and by the resulting capital accumulation within their community. This composite dynamic has, in a handful of years, reshaped the whole nature, look and structure of the neighborhood.

One final note is required here. The change in economic activities among the Turkish community was an effect of a rapid demographic transformation that created economic opportunities: money could be earned in renting accommodation to newly immigrated people from all over the world. Superdiversity, so to speak, became a superb opportunity for emancipation, empowerment and economic prosperity among the Turkish community. It enabled sudden class mobility and class restratification.

This process of restratification is not yet finished; on the contrary, the economic symbiosis between older and new groups of immigrants is perpetually deepened and widened. The new businesses operated by members of the Turkish community employ significant numbers of new immigrants. The industrial cleaning business hires people 'off the street' for cleaning jobs; the general contractor, the DIY and the supermarkets likewise offer employment – temporary, low-skilled and not generously remunerated employment – to newcomers who are in need of money. Supply trucks of Turkish supermarkets are offloaded by Bulgarian and Russian men; African and Latin-American women are recruited for occasional cleaning jobs; and all do their shopping in the small groceries and night shops as well as in the more upscale supermarkets.

These newcomers thus offer the upwardly mobile Turkish-origin business elite a flexible reserve army of labor and so form a vital factor for achieving success – an elastic market of cheap labor. In addition, these processes show that what I called 'ethnic enterprise' earlier, can, in fact, be seen as a more porous and heterogeneous phenomenon, in which different groups collaborate in a hierarchy of labor and opportunity. Even if the basic relationship – we can safely assume – is one of pretty grim exploitation, it has at the same time an effect of social and economic, systemic cohesion. Groups that are socio-economically differently positioned nevertheless depend on each other and maintain close interactions with each other, usually in the kind of 'ecumenical' Dutch we encountered earlier, and in an ambiance of what we could qualify as conviviality or moderate solidarity: 'scratch my back and I'll scratch yours'.

Unfinished Transitions

This transformation of the neighborhood happened surprisingly quickly; the move from working-class to upwardly mobile professional middle-class took many new entrepreneurs a mere handful of years; the same short time was needed for members of the Turkish community to adapt their houses to the endless demand for cheap rental accommodation and gather substantial capital that way. This rapid transformation intersected with a slower one: the emergence of a professional and highly skilled middle-class among the younger members of the Turkish community. From an average immigrant neighborhood, the area has now rapidly grown into some kind of an ethnic middle-class home, in which professional and social ambitions are conspicuously displayed.

What we see here, consequently, is a newly emerging structure, a very recent one that is still very much in the process of becoming. Language can, again, illuminate the complex, ambivalent and evolving nature of this process.

I mentioned earlier that the younger and more highly qualified members of the Turkish community are fluent bilinguals, proficient both in their Turkish home language and the advanced levels of Dutch proficiency that follow from higher education qualifications. One of the features of the new and more ambitious forms of economic activity by these younger members of immigrant groups is that they explicitly target what we can call an 'ecumenical' audience. Even if they bear a sometimes explicit ethnic character and even if most of their customers would be members of the same ethnic group, publicly displayed signs would almost invariably be in Dutch. Exceptions would still operate in Turkish–Dutch bilingual codes. Dutch clearly dominates the signs in the new service industries owned by the new Turkish middle-class professionals. Consider Figure 5.3.

We see part of the window of a shop offering financial services: mortgages, accounting services, insurance and consumer credit. The information on the window is neatly organized in symmetrical bilingualism: Turkish text on the left, Dutch text on the right. The thing is, however, that the Dutch text contains a glaring orthographic error. 'Hipothecaire lening' (mortgage) should be 'Hypothecaire lening', with a 'y' instead of an 'i'. Similar errors in Dutch can be seen on other shop windows of more ambitious businesses in the neighborhood. Thus, for instance, the recently started Turkish-owned industrial cleaning firm advertises 'industriële onderhoud' (industrial cleaning), where 'industrieel onderhoud' would be more in line with standard Dutch. Those are emblematic features of 'immigrant accent' in Dutch, effects of bilingualism and language contact that appear to persist

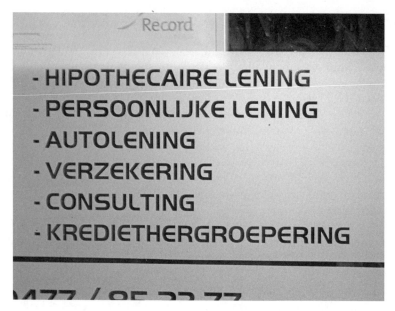

Figure 5.3 'Hipothecaire lening'

in spite of generally very high levels of Dutch proficiency among more highly qualified young members of the Turkish community.

We thus begin to see the ambivalence and fractality of the process of transformation. An 'old' immigrant (and class) accent enters into a new evolving economic and class stratum, testifying to the unfinished and ongoing character of the becoming of a new ethnic middle-class. We see the emergence of a new order, but some defining traces of the old order are still there. We see, for instance, how a *general* re-stratification – the rise of an ethnic middle-class in a formerly working-class and immigrant area – is accompanied by a *specific* reiteration of older class-stratificating features: the persistence of 'immigrant accent', seen as 'sub-standard' and thus capable of becoming a fractal stratifier *within* the ethnically diverse middle-class in the neighborhood.

It is not unlikely that we should understand the use of Dutch in these new businesses as an expression of the fluent bilingualism of the new young entrepreneurs; we can also (and simultaneously) see it as a gesture of aspiration and ambition, characterizing the upwardly mobile by means of 'language display' (in the sense of Eastman & Stein, 1993) and expressing the desire to draw customers from all groups in the area. Dutch selects the widest possible audience in the neighborhood; the use of Dutch signals that all are welcome.

This attempt towards language display, however, is unsuccessful – the emblematic immigrant accent shines through – and in addition, we will see presently that the Dutch displayed here fits into a broader category of 'ecumenical' Dutch signs. Dutch is the most accurate diagnostic of the way in which the rapid social transformations in the neighborhood proceed.

Ecumenical Dutch as a Diagnostic

The reason for this is that the ecumenical orientation in signage, expressed in the use of Dutch, is not restricted to new elite businesses in the neighborhood. We will encounter and discuss it as a feature of new churches in the next chapter, and we already emphasized in Chapter 4 that varieties of Dutch are the lingua franca of the neighborhood. Consequently, whenever businesses address a broad audience, they would use Dutch – or at least approximative varieties that could be read and understood as Dutch. Consider Figures 5.4 and 5.5.

In Figures 5.4 and 5.5 we see signs in shops that are distinctly non-elite. In Figure 5.4, the shop in question is owned by an Albanian man, and specializes in repairs of all kinds of electrical appliances; it also sells

Figure 5.4 'Alles elektro'

Figure 5.5 'Dezen persoon'

bottom-of-the-range used appliances very cheaply: repaired TV sets, refrigerators, stoves. It is, thus, typically a shop catering for new immigrants with not much cash to spend on household equipment, and the shop is using the volatility of residence patterns as a crucial business condition. People sometimes have to leave their homes quickly and urgently need to sell their equipment to, among others, the Albanian repair shop. That shop, in turn, can sell those used goods cheaply to newcomers urgently in need of appliances; the shop owners can also repair damaged hand-me-downs given to newcomers. This shop is typically an infrastructure catering for the very specific needs of a superdiverse neighborhood.

The same goes for the shop documented in Figure 5.5. This shop is owned by a Turkish couple and sells cheap textile – curtains, towels, sheets and blankets – as well as some other household items such as glasses and cups, pots and pans and cutlery. Like the repair shop, it would be a shop that attracts customers from the lower end of the market: people who need to quickly and cheaply furnish their house or apartment and turn it into a pleasant home at modest expense. Again, this is obviously not an elite business. Yet, both shops use Dutch signage; but let us take a closer look.

In Figure 5.4, the shop window announces 'alles elektro reparatie'. Many would identify this as pidgin Dutch; almost nothing in these three words is in accordance with Dutch linguistic and spelling norms. A more normative version of this would be 'Alle electro reparaties', with a plural noun 'reparaties' with a corresponding inflected adjective 'alle', and with 'electro' written with 'c' rather than with 'k'. Remarkably, a complex noun such as 'huishoudtoestellen' (household appliances) is spelled correctly. But the shop also promises 'zes manden garantie' – translated as 'six *baskets* of guarantee', because 'manden' (baskets) should have been 'maanden' (months).

We see in Figure 5.4 an attempt at writing Dutch manifestly hampered by severe constraints on access to normative varieties of written Dutch. Notwithstanding these constraints, Dutch is used here because it is the ecumenical lingua franca in the neighborhood. Potential customers from this shop do not belong to one specific group or community; they can come from any corner of the world. The safest and most neutral code to address this superdiverse population is in Dutch – *any* form of Dutch. And while the people who manufactured the lettering on the shop window were obviously well skilled in graphic techniques, standard Dutch orthography was clearly not within their purview.

The same applies to Figure 5.5. The handwritten sign on the window was accompanied by stills from a surveillance camera, showing pictures of a man – probably a shoplifter – and the sign reads 'wie kent dezen persoon en weet waar hij woond' ('who knows this person and knows where he lives'). Like in the previous example, this sign shows several orthographic problems. 'Dezen persoon' would have been correct until the 1950s, when the orthographic rules of Dutch were changed and where 'deze persoon' (without final 'n' in the demonstrative 'deze') became normative. And 'woond' should be 'woont', with a 't' and not with a 'd'. This is an ad-hoc sign, a temporary message posted because of an emergency; it is safe to assume that this is handwritten by the shop owner and that it reflects his/her degree of fluency in written Dutch. Like in Figure 5.4, we see how a social stratum is reflected into a sign: this is sub-elite Dutch, Dutch with a thick immigrant accent, and it reflects the position of its authors in the social stratification of the neighborhood.

At the bottom end of the spectre of ecumenical Dutch, we encounter signs such as Figure 5.6.

This sign was posted on the window of an internet shop operated by people from the Indian subcontinent. Internet shops, obviously, cater for the lowest segment of the market in the area: people who have no official address and who have, therefore, no access to subscription internet. It is impossible to determine the 'language' in which country names such as 'Sut Africa' (South Africa), 'Tunesea' (Tunisia) and 'Turky' (Turkey) are written. It is, however, possible to determine the origins of 'Peiro' (Peru): it is written in

Figure 5.6 'Peiro'

the Antwerp dialect, the local native vernacular variety of Dutch in which [e:] would be pronounced as [ae:], a sound which is written as 'ei'. The dynamics of access, and the constraints on access to language varieties is obvious here: the people who wrote this sign lack almost any form of access to normative varieties of Dutch; thus, they draw from an informal well of 'how it sounds' and convert this in a sort of eye dialect.

One final example is useful here, because it underscores the compelling dominance of ecumenical Dutch. Figure 5.7 shows signage on a recently closed shop.

Almost everything in the signs displayed here is in Dutch. The main sign announces that the shop has moved to another area; in announcing that, the authors write 'verhuist' instead of 'verhuisd' ('moved') – an emblematic ortho-graphic error in Dutch, in which orthographic difference between 'd' and 't' signals an inflectional feature and not an acoustic one: the notorious 'd–t rule'.

Intriguingly, the commodity previously traded in that shop was *language*. The business was operated by a small group of young men of Moroccan descent, and they offered driving lessons *in Arabic*, in preparation for the Belgian driver's license test, specifically targeting Moroccan women recently arrived in Belgium. While the driver's license tests are in Dutch, lessons in Arabic can significantly facilitate things for Moroccan-born customers

Figure 5.7 Arabic driver's license

whose Dutch is elementary. After a few months, and in an attempt to broaden their customer base, the business moved to an area more densely populated by Moroccan immigrants. The thing is that this business deals explicitly in services in a language other than Dutch, but that almost all the signage on the window is in Dutch – from the opening hours down to the schedule of classes and the announcement of the transfer to a different location. Manifestly, ecumenical Dutch is not just an option in this neighborhood: it is something of a default, a 'point zero' in public communication.

The list of examples is virtually endless; as I mentioned earlier, the sociolinguistic stratification in this neighborhood is not just a hierarchy among languages; it is also a hierarchy *within* languages, notably within Dutch. Two remarks should be added to this.

First, in spite of the sometimes catastrophic orthographic challenges posed by some of the signs, they *effectively communicate*. Dutch, as we know, is the ecumenical medium of communication in the neighborhood. Consequently, it is used there in a bewildering range of varieties, and audiences display a quite remarkable elasticity and tolerance when it comes to understanding misspelled forms. Very few people would have difficulties understanding that 'Peiro' stands for 'Peru', or 'Sut Africa' for 'South Africa'; the same goes for the handwritten emergency note and the 'Alles elektro reparatie' sign. Dutch has an ecumenical function in the area, and it therefore appears in ecumenical varieties – very few of them satisfactory in the eyes of any school teacher of standard Dutch, but most, if not all, of them pragmatically adequate for the purposes they need to serve. In fact, the neighborhood can be said to be characterized by *precisely this ecumenical Dutch*. Its emergence and density is a defining feature of the development of the neighborhood into a superdiverse one; it is, in other words, a defining part of the recently evolved language regime of the area.

Two, this ecumenical Dutch signals newly evolving as well as perduring structures in the neighborhood. Remarkably, the sub-elite examples in Figures 5.4 to 5.7 belong, in essence, to the same sociolinguistic and indexical category as that in Figure 5.3 (the financial services business), even if differences in degree appear: they are all 'Dutch with an immigrant accent', and seeing these accented signs instantly identifies the author as an immigrant. Thus, the use of ecumenical Dutch connects the shopkeepers at the very bottom of the market to the new elite entrepreneurs who use Dutch in their shop signs as well. The rapid socio-economic and class restratification we witness in the area does not seem to be synchronized with a sociocultural restratification; the 'old' cultural features of social position – accented Dutch – occur pervasively across very different social strata now; they are a *durée* phenomenon.

This is where we see the unfinished character of the processes observable in the neighborhood: certain signs mark a dramatic and sharp upward social mobility for some groups; the same signs, however, also mark their 'belonging' in an older stratification, so to speak. And that anachronism characterizes both the dynamics of the social system here, as well as its constraints and obstacles – we see the engines that propel people towards higher social positions, but we see, simultaneously, the factors that slow them down. Different historicities and different historical forces can be read from the same types of signs here, and as we noted at the outset, their appearance in synchronic space does not suggest just *one* thing: it suggests complex processes in which push and pull factors interact. By attending to their complexity, such signs serve as an excellent diagnostic of what goes on below the surface as well as on the surface. If fact, we begin to understand that they are pretty astonishingly accurate chronicles of complexity.

The Historical Image of the Neighborhood

We can see how our ethnographic linguistic landscaping enables us to (a) compose a detailed image of the synchronic order present in the neighborhood and (b) to read from and through this synchronic image the traces of various asynchronous processes of becoming. We see multiple histories coincide into a 'synchronized' space, we see different coinciding speeds of change operating on the same process, and anachronisms marking the unfinished character of these different processes of transformation.

Two concluding remarks are in order now; one with respect to how this detailed and analytic image of the neighborhood corresponds to widespread popular images of the neighborhood. This will be the topic of this section; in the next section, I will comment on the ways in which we can see the complex, dynamic and evolving organization of the neighborhood as a form of order, more precisely: as an essential infrastructure for superdiversity. The two remarks are obviously connected to each other.

We have seen earlier that the neighborhood is known to urban planners and policy makers as a 'problematic' one. In all the critical statistics, the area scores above or below average. Objectively, this is a poor neighborhood.

Subjectively as well: in the perception of many of the native inhabitants – both the older working-class ones *and* the more recently immigrated middle-class people – the neighborhood is perceived as deteriorating. That is, many people see the direction of change in this neighborhood as uniform and linear: it is on its way down, period. Very often this perception is built on idealized images of the past, when the Statiestraat–Driekoningenstraat was widely known as an area of proud and self-confident commerce, character-ized by the typically cosy atmosphere of inner-city working class culture, and as a place where good money could be earned with honest business. The image of the street and the broader area nowadays, in contrast, is that of an ongoing process of decay and degradation, instantiated by the large numbers of new immigrants, internet and night shops, and emblematic façades such as the one in Figure 5.8.

In Figure 5.8, we see traces of the original Dutch name of the shop ('Hobby-Creatief', a hobby and handicraft shop); we also see a second histori-cal layer, though: 'Danisman', the name of the Turkish owner who sold the shop some years ago to a couple from Gujarat. From Dutch, over Turkish to Gujarati: this 'cascade' symbolizes the decay of the area to many of its native inhabitants, from the native Belgians of long ago, to the Turkish people until recently, to the newcomers whose origins are often unknown to the inhabit-ants – even if they are customers of this shop. Appearances such as these summarize complex histories into one layered image that can be read as a chronicle of degradation.

The native population of the area are, unsurprisingly, the ones who have most influence with the local authorities, and after a protracted lobbying campaign an ambitious renovation scheme was implemented a few years ago

Figure 5.8 The Gujarati grocery

in the Statiestraat–Driekoningenstraat. The street was completely rebuilt and turned into a one-way traffic street so as to reduce noise pollution; the sidewalks were made broader and more attractive; and nicely tiled stone benches were placed at regular intervals. The whole operation cost millions and was explicitly aimed at attracting 'better' shops to the area – meaning: shops owned by native Belgians and selling boutique commodities. In conjunction with that effort, the city authorities also repeatedly cracked down on the night shops, internet and betting shops in the area, claiming that they were sites of contraband, drugs and human trafficking. The whole period of 'improvement' was experienced by many as an attempt towards ethnic and class cleansing – an effort towards restoring the area to its old glory, towards *embourgeoisement*.

Naturally, this was a failure. No 'better' shops opened their doors, and one reason was that the reconstruction of the street and the sidewalks had sharply reduced the parking spaces in the area. Some of the 'better' shops in the area closed their doors though, anticipating a long period of public works affecting their income. The renovation of the street, consequently, turned things for the worse in the eyes of those who had campaigned for it. The new sidewalks and benches are happily used by the superdiverse population of the area, leading to the unwelcome result that native middle-class passers-by now have to cut through groups of recognizably foreign people (usually men) outside betting shops and cafés, smoking their cigarettes and chatting while comfortably sitting on the new and fancy benches – precisely the sort of traumatic experience that leads to 'feelings of unsafety' in certain strands of the public opinion.

While the looks of the street have dramatically improved, the social texture of its population has not been affected by it. And the City Council has not achieved its goal of gentrifying the neighborhood by attracting native-owned commerce to the area. Yet, we have seen that there are signs of gentrification in the neighborhood – very important and massive signs. There is, first, the immigration of a new class of affluent, young native middle-class professionals buying houses in the neighborhood. Also the rise and consolidation of an ethnic professional middle-class has affected the dynamics of the whole area, creating a new 'center' of entirely different socio-economic occupations than before. Remember Figure 5.2, where we saw a Turkish-owned pita and chips shop right next to a Turkish-owned law firm: even by the exacting standards of the City Council, surely this must be a sign of 'improvement'?

These signs went unnoticed, though. They were not as clearly readable as the one in Figure 5.8 – images of decay are apparently always more powerful than images of improvement. Very few native people in the area pause to consider the changes in the neighborhood, unless when such changes can be seen as negative. Very few people, in fact, *know* about these changes. The gradual but unending transformation of the neighborhood, detectable through small indices spread over the whole of the area, appears to hit a blind spot – which testifies to the pervasive preference in our thinking for linear and simple models of development, the kind of simple linearity that can be read, one supposes, from Figure 5.8. People do not easily notice the complex and multifiliar patterns that run through their own social environments. And even if they notice them, they appear to reduce them to simple schemata of development. Entropy in action.

Infrastructures for Superdiversity

When the complexity of the environment is effectively perceived and understood, an entirely different picture of the area emerges. We can now see that in the rapidly changing and unfinished processes of transformation of the neighborhood, one maxim seems to be present: changes and transformations are governed by the need for an adequate infrastructure for the people who live there. And if that aggregate community is complex and dynamic, so will the infrastructure be. There is not one infrastructure in the neighborhood, there are several overlapping and complementary ones, all of which cater for segments of the neighborhood's population of varying size and structure. The neighborhood in its totality can be seen as *a layered complex of infrastructures for superdiversity*, and all sorts of delicate interactions and relationships are constructed in and through these infrastructures. This infrastructural dimension, in fact, is probably the 'order' in the 'chaos' of the neighborhood. It is the complex logic that ties together the seemingly incoherent dynamics of the place, the apparently contradictory forces that operate on it, and the absence of uniformity it displays.

We have seen that the neighborhood is composed of groups that are ethnically and socio-economically very different. Certain facilities in the neighborhood will be specific to certain groups, while others are more general in their scope. The publicly visible signs often already inform us of the preferential audiences; ethnographic immersion in them tells us the other half of the story. Let us begin by looking at some of the specific ones and work our way towards the more ecumenical ones.

(a)   The category of people lowest on the socio-economic ladder are the recent immigrants; they are very often residing in the neighborhood as undocumented immigrants; they can therefore not get an official address, no local bank account and no subscription to telephone or internet providers. Internet shops and shops handling money transfer services are therefore typically infrastructures that cater for this group of inhabitants. Apart from an occasional outsider entering an internet shop to buy cigarettes or soft drinks, few people outside of this category would use such facilities.

(b)   The same goes evidently for the local housing market, which is typically segmented into different categorical strata. On the one end, we would have the cheap and basic studios and flats rented out to newcomers; on the other end we would have sometimes ostentatious middle-class houses with gardens, typically sold to, and stylishly transformed by, native, young middle-class couples. Cross-overs are very rare, since market elasticity only works in one direction. But the availability of a flexible supply of cheap accommodation, located closely to important axes of mobility – the railway station, the highway – turns the neighborhood into a magnet for newcomers.

(c)   These newcomers would also typically be the main customers of the shops we illustrated in Figures 5.4 and 5.5: places where cheap furniture, textiles, food and household appliances can be bought – cheap enough to pay cash – and where used or damaged commodities can be repaired and maintained. The handful of launderettes in the area would also fit this category. This 'budget economy' is a very conspicuous presence in the neighborhood, and some of it is also ecumenical: some chain franchises of the cheaper kind are located in the area, and they attract customers from all segments of the neighborhood.

(d) The cafés and betting shops are also quite specific in the audiences they draw. In spite of the overwhelming dominance of Dutch in public signs, most of the cafés would be 'specialized', so to speak, and address particular ethnic groups. The Polish, Russian and Bulgarian people visit different cafés than the Turkish people and the Belgian ones.

(e) Hair saloons would also be rather clearly ethnically specialized, though the picture is not uniform. There is a very high density of Turkish and Moroccan hair salons in the area – in the broader Antwerp area, Moroccans even refer to a distinct 'Berchem style' of haircut. Their customers would come mainly from the same communities. But some Turkish and Moroccan hair saloons attract customers from all segments of the population (I myself use the services of an excellent Moroccan barber). The Belgian hairdresser, considerably more distinguished in appearance than his Turkish or Moroccan competitors, works mainly for a native (and also non-local) clientele, including the better-off Eastern European ladies who are served by a Polish and a Russian assistant in the shop.

(f) The segmentation we saw in cafés does not count for restaurants. The area has a high density of Turkish restaurants, ranging from basic pita and chips bars, to more elaborate pizza or specialty restaurants. They attract business from all segments of the neighborhood. Some are quite popular among students attending the secondary school in the neighborhood – delicious and affordable snacks can be purchased for lunch there.

(g) The same goes for night shops. They are usually owned and operated by new immigrants, but their customer base is very broad. Food, alcohol and tobacco can be purchased there until the early hours of the morning.

(h) And for the groceries, both small ones and the supermarket-size ones. There is a superb daily supply of fresh vegetables and fruits, and plenty of choice. All segments of the population go there. The quite numerous bakeries in the area (almost all owned by Moroccan and Turkish bakers) also work ecumenically. And while the Belgian butcher in the area supplies primarily Belgian customers, the two Moroccan ones sell their produce to anyone.

(i) The more specialized 'ethnic' businesses – the doctor, the dentist, the lawyers and financial services providers – mostly cater for audiences from their own ethnic community. One of the lawyers, however, is a community leader representing the Berchem area in the City Council.

(j)   Pharmacies, medical doctors, banks and other established service suppliers operate for everyone in the neighborhood. The same goes for the schools in the area, the welfare offices, social employment offices and the branch of the local administration and police.

(k)   A special role is played by the providers of building and construction materials and services. The Hakan DIY is probably the most ecumenical shop in the area, attracting customers from all walks of life. The same goes for a native-owned hardware shop, where just a slight predominance of native customers can be noted. The industrial cleaning firm and the building contractor operate in a more regional market.

We begin to see a highly intricate web of relationships between the various infrastructures in the area, a specific sort of order. Some facilities are primarily used by small and specific groups of people, with income differences as the major diacritic; but many are used by all. Ethnic and class lines are crossed continuously, there are numerous meeting points in the area and invisible lines tying separate groups together in transactions and other forms of engagement; and the availability of cheap food, fresh bread and vegetables seven days per week is not just good for low-income people, but also a happy aspect of life for the middle-class inhabitants. The same goes for night shops: middle-class Belgians who get an unexpected visitor at night can still fetch a decent bottle of wine or a selection of special Belgian beers from the night shops and avoid social embarrassment that way.

Note, nonetheless, that this class-crossing elasticity, as a rule, only works in one direction: the middle class has access to the totality of the infrastructures; people lower on the socio-economic ladder experience financial obstacles and have access only to a (cheaper) segment of those infrastructures. The aspect of class stratification within this system is easy to overlook, yet it is important.

The relationships between the various segments of the population in the neighborhood are, thus, multifaceted, structured and intense, and they contribute to a level of social cohesion and conviviality that stands in sharp contrast to the public image of the area. Violent crime is rare, and incidents trigger great inter-ethnic solidarity. When a specialized chocolate shop, owned by Belgian–Italian people, went up in fire a handful of years ago, the shop owners and their children were rescued and evacuated by their Turkish neighbors; a fire disaster in a Turkish-owned supermarket likewise provoked a wave of solidarity and spontaneous support across the neighborhood. The Gujarati grocer borrows the Belgian newspapers from his neighbor, a

Moroccan hairdresser; and a night shop owned by a man from Afghanistan sells every possible variety of Polish beers and vodka because his neighbors are Polish construction workers. As mentioned, new immigrants can find temporary and low-paid jobs in the flourishing new businesses in the neighborhood. There is no reason to paint this particular kind of relationship in romantic colors, for we have seen the class-stratifying aspects of this, but it is a relationship of mutual dependency nonetheless, conflictual at one level and peaceful on another level.

This general level of peaceful coexistence I call 'conviviality', and I would suggest we see it as a form of order at one scale level. It is the scale evel at which people agree to 'live and let live' and express a distaste for violence and overt conflicts in social relationships. It is expressed by the phenomenal amount of so-called 'phatic' activities that people perform and in which they express a desire for friendliness while they express apparently trivial joint concerns – the hairdresser talking about the weather to me, the butcher asking whether I am on my way to some event because I am wearing a necktie, and so on. We have grown accustomed to seeing such 'phatic' activities as essentially meaningless, as things people do just to keep the channels of communication open and clear. I would suggest we see it as *very* relevant, as a really important *structure* of social life through which people manage to agree and get on with each other in spite of deep inequalities and bewildering diversity. Conviviality is the attitude that enables people to accept different trajectories of life and different ways of going about things within the same space, and creates a level of sharedness that can generate solidarity and sympathy with others. It is not a detail, therefore, and not trivial and meaningless, but a highly meaningful mode of conduct.

Places of worship play a significant role in the neighborhood infrastructure too, as we shall see in the next chapter. By addressing churches as one specific type of infrastructure in the next chapter, I hope at the same time to provide a synthesis of the various points that had to be spread over two different chapters and various sections for reasons of clarity. We can now integrate our analysis and bring it to bear on one particular object of inquiry: churches.

6 The Vatican of the Diaspora

'There should be twice the number of churches', a pastor from Nigeria told me, 'We just can't satisfy the demand here'. The pastor was responding to my question, why there were so many new churches in my neighborhood. According to him, we can expect an increase in religious activities here, because:

> so many people are lonely and have no community here (...) and they look for support – they get material support elsewhere, but they come here because they also need spiritual support and hope.

The number of such people is rising, he emphasized, and they are not by any means confined to immigrants. His own congregation, about 50 strong, consists of 'people from everywhere' – Africans as well as Europeans from Antwerp, but also from Brussels, France, The Netherlands. He was currently enlarging the one room (already a joined living room and garage) in which he held his services, because the congregation expanded continuously, and since he started his church in 2004 he had never seen such a rapid increase in interest.

The Nigerian pastor is one out of a good number of evangelical priests who have set up churches in my neighborhood. The arrival, success and continuous activity of evangelical churches is the single most remarkable change in the social space of my neighborhood over the last five to six years. Indeed, churches have become one of the main infrastructures of superdiversity there.

I have followed the development of these churches with growing interest, and for quite a while, they have been one of the foci of my ongoing inquiries in my neighborhood. Let us take a closer look at these fascinating places.

Worshipping in 16 Places

On 5 May 2011, I counted 16 places of worship in my neighborhood. I am mentioning the date for a reason: the patterns of presence and visibility of the places of worship change rapidly and continuously; hence the present number is different from past and future ones. The Statiestraat, as we know, used to be a flourishing commercial center; over the past decade, however, numerous small businesses and shops have terminated their activities and the neighborhood counts a large number of vacant commercial premises available at relatively modest prices.[1] New churches, consequently, rent former shops on a short-term basis, then move to another (larger) one before they take a more permanent lease and begin to rebuild the premises. We shall see examples of this itinerary below.

The 16 places of worship are divided as follows.

- Two Catholic churches.
- Three mosques (one Turkish, one Moroccan, one international).
- 11 evangelical churches:
  - one local;
  - five African;
  - three Brazilian;
  - two Latin American.

The Catholic churches are evidently the oldest ones in the neighborhood. The St Willibrord Church is a listed monument and its oldest parts were built in the 15th century; the St Hubertus Church (the largest building in the neighborhood, located in the heart of the Statiestraat–Driekoningenstraat area) was built in the early 20th century. Both churches used to serve large congregations of parishioners until a couple of decades ago. Currently, the picturesque St Willibrord Church remains a frequently used venue for weddings, funerals, holy communions and other religious events. The two churches, however, had to be amalgamated into one parish and together offer three-weekly services to a sharply reduced and changed congregation. The Sunday service at St Hubertus currently attracts some 30 faithful, a large majority of whom are Filipino families with their children, and single Polish men. The weekly services are still held in Dutch; in other parishes in Antwerp, services are now held in French, English, Polish and Russian owing to the overwhelming numerical dominance of immigrant faithful from Central Africa, the Philippines, Poland and Byelorussia.

Chronologically, the three mosques are second in line. The Turkish Kuba mosque is by far the largest owing to the preponderance of Turkish immigrants in the neighborhood. The mosque owns a large complex of buildings in a side-street of the Statiestraat, and organizes Saturday Qur'an classes, as well as some special religious and cultural events along with the regular religious services. The Moroccan El Mouhsinine mosque in a side-street of the Driekoningenstraat is far smaller and a few years younger than the Turkish one. Both mosques attract their faithful almost exclusively from the neighborhood, they are strictly local places of worship. The newest mosque in the neighborhood is the Al Zahra mosque, also located in a side-street of Driekoningenstraat. This small shi'ite mosque attracts an international audience and is not affiliated to either the Turkish or the Moroccan Muslim networks in the Antwerp area. Extreme-right and Zionist sources allege that the mosque is a center of Hezbollah activity in Antwerp. Note that these three mosques are the only ones in the whole district of Berchem. My neighborhood is the center for Muslim religious activity in the wider area. All three mosques are housed in ordinary houses, sometimes extended and rebuilt, but hardly noticeable for the uninterested passer-by.

The local evangelical church in a side-street of Driekoningenstraat was started by a Canadian couple in 1972 and has grown into a flourishing congregation of mostly local members. The international ones, by contrast are a phenomenon of the past decade; a superdiversity phenomenon. All these churches are housed in former commercial premises – they are 'shop window churches' of varying size. The smallest among them have a safety license for 49 people; the larger ones for 99; and one church is currently expanding its building so as to host several hundreds of worshippers. Note that all of them comply with city and district regulations on public buildings – they do attend to the paperwork for building, safety and hygiene.

The new evangelical churches have their origins in Africa (five churches, notably from Ghana and Nigeria), Brazil (three churches) and Latin America (two churches). One of the Brazilian churches sub-lets its facilities to two African churches; another Nigerian church uses the premises of a Latin-American church.

We shall turn to the new churches in some detail below. But before that, let us draw attention to one general point about the landscape of religious places in this neighborhood.

Visibility and Invisibility

We know that the Catholic churches in the neighborhood are very visible: they define the neighborhood and even give their names to streets, squares and communities. Yet, these highly visible places of worship have lost their stable, large local constituencies and now draw on a small immigrant and fluid community of faithful. The Catholic churches, one could say, are empty, they are not really in business. The successful ones, by contrast,

Figure 6.1 El Mouhsinine Mosque

are all but invisible. The mosques are only known to members of their religious communities and to a small number of non-Muslim local inhabitants. Consider Figure 6.1, a picture of the El Mouhsinine mosque.

The mosque is a small house in a row, quite ordinary in outlook and only identified as a mosque by two small inscriptions in Arabic. It is painted in ocre-yellow rather than in the emblematic green of Islam. The doors of the building are only opened when there is a service; when closed, the house looks like any other in the neighborhood.

The same invisibility applies to the new evangelical churches, though we see a pattern of development there. In a first stage of implantation, the churches are hardly identifiable as such. Consider Figure 6.2.

We see the front of a building that was, until recently, a lingerie shop. To the shop window, an A4 poster is stuck (Figure 6.3), and unless one reads that poster one would not identify this place as a Brazilian church.

Finding out about the sharing of space between different churches also demands attention to small details. Figure 6.4 shows the front of a Brazilian church, clearly identified by red lettering. A small A4 poster on the window presents one of the two Ghanese churches located at the same address. An 'upstart' obviously tags his activities on to those of a more established organization here.

Figure 6.2 Former Lingerie Pascetti

Little outward fuss is made by the churches, at least not in the early
stages of their presence. They just appear to blend into the landscape, often
not bothering about removing or covering the previous owner's shop signs.
When they have established themselves, however, they do become more visibly present and identifiable as churches. The Brazilian church that originally
used the former Lingerie Pascetti recently acquired and renovated another

Figure 6.3 Ministerio Resgate in Lingerie Pascetti

building; Figure 6.5 shows the way in which this church displays itself to the outside world at present.

The largest and most successful church in the neighborhood appears to have no difficulties with being identified as such. The Nigeria-based church attracts a large constituency of several hundreds of followers from a wide area, including from France and The Netherlands, and recently successfully

Figure 6.4 Space sharing

Figure 6.5 Ministerio Resgate's new premises

Figure 6.6 Redeemed Christian Church of God

applied for a building permit to expand the former superette in which it is housed (Figure 6.6).

Some of the churches (especially the African ones) occasionally organize larger events in Antwerp hotels and event halls, led by senior preachers who travel around the network of churches. Thus, the Nigerian church seen in Figure 6.6 recently co-organized a mega-event in which a Nigerian 'Apostle' performed public healing; the Apostle can be found on YouTube performing similar healings in The Philippines, in front of an audience of thousands.

The regular presence of large numbers of worshippers from Africa and Latin America has spawned a number of exotic food shops (often announcing 'African, Asian and European' commodities), because the faithful combine shopping with the long hours of religious practice during weekend days. Even if the presence of churches has not dramatically altered the looks of the neighborhood, it has affected the neighborhood's functions and sociolinguistic landscape quite profoundly, and has had an impact on its economic structure too. The churches have yielded commercial spin-offs; their arrival and consolidation in the neighborhood has changed the whole of the neighborhood, and in more ways than just those connected to religious affiliation.

Fully Globalized Churches

The church in Figure 6.6 is a Pentecostal–Charismatic church, and Meyer (2006) provides the following characterization of these churches, drawing on observations from Ghana:

Many Pentecostal-Charismatic Churches, the latest brand of Pentecostalism that started to thrive in Ghana since the early 1990s, are run in a business-like fashion by flamboyant pastors. Making skilful use of the modern mass media that became deregulated and commercialized in the course of Ghana's turn to a democratic constitution, Pentecostal-Charismatic Churches have become omnipresent in the public sphere (. . .). Similar to American televangelism, many of them have adopted mass media so as to produce and broadcast spectacular church services to a mass audience. Recorded during church conventions yet edited carefully so as to ensure utmost credibility (. . .), such programs claim to offer eye witness accounts of the power of God to perform miracles via the charismatic pastor and his prayer force. Featured as an embodiment – indeed an 'objectification' – of divine power, the pastor conveys a sense of amazement and wonder. (Meyer, 2006: 12; see also Marshall-Fratani, 1998: 283)

The use of mass media (and increasingly social media) by this type of evangelical churches is well documented. Churches offer fictionalized accounts of God's power by means of broadcasted *telenovelas*, sold on video-cassettes or CD ROMs to faithful all over the world, along with copies of the Scripture, books of prayer and song, and collected sermons from leading pastors (see Pype, 2009, for examples from Congo; Marshall-Fratani, 1998, for Nigeria). Increasingly, Facebook groups emerge as nodes of organization for these religious communities, and social media are now fully incorporated into the media complex used by these churches.

Services in these churches take several hours and are distinctly multimodal and multimedial. There is live music, singing and dancing, and sermons and prayers broadcasted over the internet from faraway places are incorporated into the local services. One Latin-American church is affiliated to Bethel TV, a religious television channel operated from Lima, Peru; the Nigerian church in Figure 6.6 has a bookstore selling books printed in Nigeria; and the Latin-American churches all identify themselves as belonging to a worldwide missionary movement. The churches are connected to networks of like-minded churches both regionally and internationally in one large complex of globalized late-modern evangelism, and the traveling 'stars' of these churches preach all over the world. The charisma of such religious movements is 'portable', in Meyer's terms:

> Pentecostalism, with its emphasis on a 'mobile self' and a 'portable charismatic identity', is a religion that speaks to experiences of dislocation, fragmentation and increasing mobility. (Meyer, 2006: 29; also Maskens, 2008)

The appearance of Pentecostal–Charismatic churches in a superdiverse neighborhood such as this one can, thus, be related to members' experiences of superdiversity – isolation, the lack of networks and communities, the need for support from such networks and communities. I will return to this topic below.

The services are also all distinctly 'spectacular' in Meyer's terminology. The presence of the Holy Spirit is invoked and allegedly experienced by participants:

> Pentecostal services are powerful sensational forms that seek to involve believers in such a way that they sense the presence of God in a seemingly *immediate* manner, and are amazed by His power. Still the Holy Spirit does not arrive out of the blue. I have witnessed many such services, in which the pastor and congregation pray for the Holy Spirit to come. After some time, the prayers become louder and louder, and many start speaking in tongues. This is taken as a sign that the Holy Spirit is manifest. At a certain moment the pastor indicates the end of the prayer session, and calls upon the Holy Spirit to heal the sick, protect the vulnerable, and expel demonic spirits. (Meyer, 2006: 11–12)

People can bring a wide variety of problems to the services. This is the list provided by one of the Brazilian churches:

> Addiction, depression, unemployment, immigration, nervosity, family, envy, hearing voices, diseases, seeing ghosts, fear, sleeplessness, death wish, voodoo, Satanism.

Whoever suffers from this interesting range of afflictions can call upon the congregation for prayer, redemption and healing. Personal testimony is very much part of the proceedings, as is speaking in tongues. And when the services are over, food and beverages are offered, and people stay in the hall for a long time after the end of the service proper. Apart from the problems listed above, people can also find a cure for loneliness and isolation in the churches.

While the churches have their roots in specific parts of the world, and would still draw most of their followers from emigrés from the same parts, they identify themselves explicitly as ecumenical, and do so by means of the choice of language in communicating with the public. But this proceeds in stages – we see history through language once again here. That the primary audience would be people from the church's area of origin can be judged from Figure 6.7; a notice stuck on the door of a Latin-American church informing followers that the leadership will be absent. The notice is in Spanish only – the projected audience for such messages is consequently Spanish-speaking. Note in passing the globalization aspect of the notice: the local leaders have gone to a meeting of the European branches of their church in Brussels.

The same church, however, identifies itself in Spanish and Dutch and welcomes Dutch-speaking potential followers (Figure 6.8).

Such ecumenism is no doubt characteristic of missionary move-ments (and recall that these churches explicitly self-identify as 'mission-ary' churches). But the *emergent* and often *unfinished* character of such

Figure 6.7 Spanish notice in a Latin-American church

Figure 6.8 Bilingual announcements on a Latin-American church

multilingual communication patterns shows, as in many of the examples discussed in Chapter 5, that this ecumenism probably represents a stage in a gradual process of implantation and solidification, in which churches initially start small and modestly, inviting primarily people with whom they share national or regional backgrounds. The inconspicuous accommodation of newly arrived churches would corroborate this. Churches start almost invisibly and work for 'home' congregations. Once these faithful have been recruited, the churches discover that there may be a broader 'market', and they start using Dutch, the language that has most currency in that area even as a transcultural vernacular, which is why I called it ecumenical Dutch earlier.

That this is in all likelihood an ad-hoc, local adaptation to circumstances rather than the work of well-oiled global religious businesses can be observed from the frequent struggles with written Dutch observable in public notices. The fine details of these processes of transformation, once more, can be read off linguistic landscaping data. Figure 6.9 shows us the poster on which a Brazilian church describes the (earlier-quoted) range of problems that can be addressed during services, along with the hours of the weekly services. The notice is in Brazilian Portuguese (right) and a highly unstable form of Dutch (left).

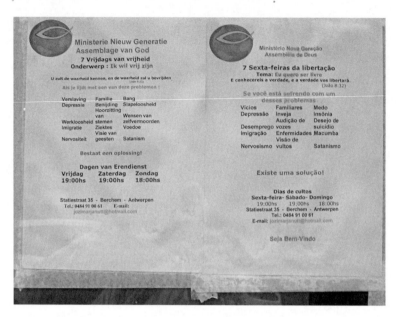

Figure 6.9 Dutch–Portuguese bilingualism in a Brazilian church

The 'Assembly of God' becomes 'God's Assemblage' in Dutch; 'hearing' in 'hearing voices' is converted into 'hoorziting', the word used for forensic and legal 'hearings' (as in immigration cases), and so forth: the Dutch in Figure 6.9 is the emergent, profoundly non-native ecumenical Dutch we encountered so often before, pointing to an absence of available resources for producing 'correct' Dutch within the church community. Concretely: when the church leadership designed this notice, they had no people fluent in Dutch literacy in their congregation yet. The poster was drawn *before* Dutch-speaking followers joined the congregation.

We can now begin to see a developmental pattern of sociocultural presence in the neighborhood, organized around gradually transforming religious sociocultural practices. The churches moved into the neighborhood quickly and re-shaped the neighborhood quite importantly in no time. In the first stage of their presence, the churches operated below the radar, using hardly noticeable spaces for organizing their activities, and targeting audiences that have their roots in a globalized regional background shared with the churches: Nigerian churches would target West-African worshippers; Brazilian ones would target Brazilians, and so forth.[2] The churches thus shape a node in a fully globalized network of religious institutions – Berchem becomes the node – and the globalized nature of the churches turns them into organizational centers for the diaspora. Diaspora groups coalesce around the churches. Missionary activity in this stage is understood as bringing together the diasporic flock of churches from the 'homeland'.

In a second stage, however, we see that the churches widen their scope of recruitment and adopt a more outward-directed strategy. Premises become more visible and conspicuous, and ecumenical languages such as Dutch now appear alongside the languages of the 'homeland', inviting worshippers that do not belong to the diasporic inner circle, so to speak. Missionary activity now becomes expressly ecumenical, and we can observe this development both in the change of the physical spaces occupied by the churches and by changes in the multilingual practices they deploy. The churches now begin to organize not just the diasporic groups, but new globalized communities wider than just the diasporic ones.

The Functions of Churches

The Pentecostal churches we have seen appear in this neighborhood have links to countries that are often seen and listed as robustly Roman-Catholic, such as Brazil and Peru. In a study of Congolese Pentecostal churches in Brussels, Maskens (2008: 49) observes that Pentecostal churches in such countries have urban origins, and that in countries such as those, their initial constituencies are made up of rural internal migrants. (Observe that Congo as well would fit the list of staunchly Roman-Catholic countries). In that sense, the churches are diaspora (or missionary) churches even in their countries of origin. Maskens points out that the fact of migration with its effects of dislocation, detachment from older local forms of social and cultural organization, the loss of an organic community and so forth, is a powerful moment of conversion (Maskens, 2008). She also notes what we have observed as well: that churches are often almost invisible (at least for some time), and she offers two explanations for this (Maskens, 2008: 50–51). (1) Many of the followers of these churches are undocumented and therefore clandestine immigrants; and (2) the churches are suspicious of the outside world, notably the Belgian State, because of the hostile climate towards 'cults' and 'sects' that was the outcome of a Belgian Parliamentary Commission inventarizing, exploring and sanctioning the activities of cults in the late 1990s. Churches that offer healing sessions are quickly perceived as cults, and such churches, consequently, 'keep their noses clean' in relation to the state.

I opened this chapter with statements from a Nigerian pastor, leader of one of the churches in the neighborhood, who pointed towards the tremendous 'market' for churches in the area. While I interviewed him, building in his church was in progress, because the 50 or so seats he could offer to worshippers no longer sufficed to accommodate the growing numbers of new converts. When asked whether his followers were from West Africa mainly, he emphasized the ecumenical nature of his church: he was attracting people from all communities in the area, and was happy to do so.[3] And as we have seen, he located the 'market' for churches such as his own in the vacant space left by the State and the local communities: people were isolated, feared they would lose God in their lives or feared to be abandoned by God because of the life they were leading, had a need for a community of 'brothers' and 'sisters' and so forth. If we want to understand the functions of these churches, we need to consider the realities of diasporic life in an area such as this one.

In earlier research performed in Brussels, we came across Pentecostal churches as well (Beyens et al., 2005), and we saw that churches such as these ones display and organize a broad range of services and forms of assistance to their followers. In fact, we concluded that such churches play a crucial role as a first-line system of informal solidarity for people whose reliance on and access to formal (state-organized) systems of solidarity was severely limited. Clandestine migrants are not eligible for welfare benefits, have no access to formal systems of social housing allocation nor to the formal labor market, and very often have restricted access to health provision, education and training programs. The church was a vital instrument for gaining access to informally allocated resources for people living in such extremely vulnerable conditions, and churches were very successful because of their low threshold of accessibility. One Congolese informant in Brussels remarked, tongue in cheek, that 'the only thing you need to do is to say that you believe in Christ' and one would gain access to a community in which one is, by definition, welcome (this point is also made by Maskens).

Churches in the neighborhood are, thus, crucial infrastructures of superdiversity; we begin to understand their presence, and their success, in terms of the complexity described in the previous chapters. Their presence makes such complexity more maneuverable for many people. In churches such as the ones described here, newcomers find a warm community, a 'family' in the words of the Nigerian pastor, of 'brothers and sisters' united by their faith in Christ. People smile when newcomers enter the group, they inquire about identity, backgrounds and living conditions, and try to help and assist wherever they can. Thus, members of such church communities can get access to cheap housing, child care, inexpensive cars and furniture, and sometimes also jobs or financial loans – all of this on the basis of informal mechanisms of solidarity that ensue, quite simply, from membership of the church community. For people who have no access to regular mechanisms of material support allocation, churches offer unique resources. Thus, the churches are not just communities of faith, but also communities of knowledge: the knowledge to survive in a hostile context, the knowledge to 'integrate' in the margins of a society such as that of contemporary Western Europe.

The ecumenism of these churches thus, could reflect not just the increased success of Pentecostal religious practice among non-diasporic groups, but also the increased vulnerability of *non*-diasporic groups as well. Clandestine immigrants are in the forefront of such processes of marginalization (Maskens, 2008: 53–54), but such processes are obviously no longer restricted to immigrants and affect a growing body of 'native' people as well, certainly in a socio-economically sub-average area such as this one. Globalized churches appear to have discovered this market, and the development in their language practices shows that they now actively recruit such new constituencies into their congregations.

The Vatican

In that way and through these mechanisms, the churches in Oud-Berchem must be seen as an emergent (and quickly consolidating) system of institutionalization and organization of solidarity among a rapidly expanding and permanently unstable social formation of people who lack access to more rigorously structured systems of solidarity. The neoliberalization of welfare and social provisions in countries such as Belgium (a process that has accelerated significantly over the past decade) has made access to services and resources increasingly competitive and selective. In order to gain access to welfare benefits, for instance, one needs an official residential address; in order to acquire that, one needs to have one's 'papers in order' and satisfy a broad, expanding and often contradictory set of criteria issued by public as well as private actors in the field of social welfare. This increasing selectivity has as an obvious effect that more and more people drop out of the systems of welfare and social service allocation, and require access to informal and low-threshold systems of allocation. Churches are highly successful 'substitute' players in this emerging field.

The fact that such churches cluster in a neighborhood such as Oud-Berchem is, consequently, probably not coincidental. As mentioned above, Oud-Berchem is both in reality and in the perception of people a poor immigrant neighborhood, populated by rapidly changing groups of short-term immigrant residents as well as by more constant residential migrant and 'native' communities. Such a neighborhood offers an infrastructure that can only be acquired in areas such as these: large amounts of cheaply available space – the former shops – and a first-line community of vulnerable people who can be potential 'customers' for religious business. People from the neighborhood flock towards such businesses, and they are joined by people from further afield, turning the neighborhood into a Vatican-like center of religious activity and its material and social spin-offs: access to a warm and welcoming community (a 'family'), to networks of mutual support and to material resources not obtainable elsewhere.

We have seen that the neighborhood offers a unique set of infrastructures for coping with the uncertainties of superdiversity; it has become a conglomerate of such infrastructures for the very diverse communities that inhabit it – not one single, clear and transparent infrastructure, but a layered and complex array of instruments that enable shifting and unstable groups of people to live there with a modicum of comfort and safety, in delicate and often unseen relationships with each other, and in a general atmosphere of conviviality. The neighborhood, I would say, is chaotic; but, as we know by now, that means that it is in order.

Notes

(1) A phone call to some real estate agents taught me that vacant commercial premises in this area can be rented at 400–600 Euro/month on average.

(2) The national or regional background of target groups is a function of the languages used by churches. The use of English enables Nigerian churches to draw in a community of followers not restricted to one country; the same goes for the use of Spanish in Latin-American churches. Portuguese restricts the target audience of Brazilian churches largely to Brazilian immigrants; hence the emergence of ecumenical Dutch, and some English, as languages that allow the recruiting of a larger constituency.

(3) In fact, when I made pictures of the house in which the church was located, a Belgian young man approached me to find out the nature of my interest. He brought me to the Nigerian pastor.

7 Conclusion: The Order of Superdiversity

It is time now to pull some of the lines in this book together and review the issues I have addressed in the different chapters.

Let me start by summarizing what I hope to have demonstrated in this book. There are two sets of arguments, one empirical, the second one methodological.

(1) The book has made a case for complexity as an empirical feature of sociolinguistic superdiversity. Superdiverse spaces, such as the one I documented in this book, can be seen as complex and stochastic systems, that is: as dynamic and non-equilibrium systems in which a variety of forces interact and very different modes of development and change can be observed. They are, to put it in the terminology I used earlier, polycentric and multifiliar – different threads simultaneously develop there, not in harmony or synchrony, but still within a broader logic of the system. This logic, I argued, is 'infrastructural'. What we see in the neighborhood is how different forms of infrastructure emerge, develop and are consolidated. These different infrastructures are tailored towards the needs of the different groups with their different needs and trajectories of residence and use; consequently, they are multiple, they form a polycentric whole. Not of isolated and separate units, however, for the infrastructures also interact across the boundaries of such groups – middle-class native people also visit the night shops and ethnic groceries, the churches have spawned several new such shops, and Turkish upwardly mobile entrepreneurs employ newly immigrated people, for instance. The end result is a particular form of order: an unstable, evolving and always 'unfinished' order, characterized by nonlinear and apparently 'chaotic' paths of ordering, stochastic moments of change creating a high level of

unpredictability to the social dynamics we can observe. Complexity is the order of superdiversity. Consequently, if we intend to address superdiversity, we have to draw away from established, modernist images of society and social process. And we need to develop tools for that, which brings me to the methodological arguments in this book.

(2) Methodologically, I argued that such complex systems can be examined by using a mixture of deep ethnographic immersion on the one hand, and an ethnographically reshaped form of LLS. The former offers us the broad and longitudinal picture of the system, the second one offers us uniquely accurate pointers towards the dynamic, polycentric or 'chaotic' structures operating within it. In particular, we needed to understand the signs that are the object of LLS as fundamentally historical – which offers us an arrow of time in our inquiries – and as tied to processes of demarcation to which various effects of power, ownership, legitimacy of usage and identity are connected. We thus see 'layered simultaneity' both in single signs as repositories and 'nexuses' of complex and 'synchronized' histories, and in the neighborhood at large. And if we wish to describe the neighborhood as a sociolinguistic system, this system is complex in the sense outlined above – polycentric, multifiliar, dynamic and so on – while widespread and popular views of that system would prefer to see it as a simple linear, 'synchronized' unit – entropic interpretations seem to dominate popular views. Complexity in the phenomenology of our object, as we have seen, meets a reduction of complexity in its interpretations. This leads to unsatisfactory analytical results, of course, and if we want to overcome these we need to shift our paradigm.

These are the two substantial sets of arguments developed in this book. They raise several additional issues, and I will spend the remainder of this chapter discussing some of them.

The discussion will be facilitated, I think, by taking a look at one final example. Figure 7.1 summarizes much of what has been said in this book, and it can serve as a lead into several fundamental reflections.

Figure 7.1 is a picture of a menu displayed on the window of a tavern called 'Bellefleur' in the Statiestraat. A 'tavern' is, in the Antwerp catering tradition, an 'improved' café, somewhat more chic than an ordinary café. It is a place where one can have a beer and coffee, as well as cake, lunch and dinner. It is typically also a place where elderly Belgian people would go in the afternoon for a cup of coffee with cake, socializing with other elderly people from the neighborhood. The interior of the Bellefleur is relatively stylish: the chairs are upholstered, there are tablecloths on the tables, and the walls are decorated with some pieces of art.

Figure 7.1 Bellefleur Tavern, menu

Bellefleur has been in operation for decades. Quite recently, the previous owners retired and the tavern was rented by a couple of Indian people – members of the new migrations that constitute the most recent and most volatile layer of residents in the neighborhood. Interestingly, the new owners did not turn the tavern into an Indian restaurant. As the menu in Figure 7.1 shows, they still advertise and offer the most traditional popular Belgian dishes – we see, for instance, 'stoofvlees met trappist' (beef stewed in trappist beer) and 'vol au vent' (stewed chicken in cream sauce), both

'Ur-Belgian' dishes. The new owners kept all the dishes that were on the earlier menu, and they still offer them to middle-aged and senior local Belgian people for lunch and dinner. They kept the original clientele of the Bellefleur intact, and one can still see, as before, elderly people chatting there over a cup of coffee with cake in the afternoon. They also kept the entire interior of the tavern intact; it is not visually identifiable as an Indian place. Behind the curtains, however, Indian newcomers are employed in the kitchen and as hired hands who run errands for the owners.

They have, however, made one alteration: they *added* new food to the menu. We see various biryani and rotty dishes advertised on the menu in Figure 7.1, and the Bellefleur now also attracts a more adventurous, younger middle-class clientele interested in exotic food. So we see how newcomers (the Indian owners) enter into a superdiverse environment, and instantly adjust to the complexities of it, on the one hand by keeping their tavern almost completely intact, thus securing continuity in clientele. On the other hand, they were able to broaden and, in a sense, redefine the tavern and its clientele as a place where younger middle-class people can have an exquisite Indian dinner. This redefinition was not done by means of a wholesale face-lift of the tavern from a traditional Antwerp tavern to an Indian specialties restaurant. No, they left the place almost entirely unchanged and just added one segment of produce to their menu. The change is in the details – an unattentive passer-by would be led to believe that Bellefleur is still exactly what it was five or seven years ago. Part of it has indeed remained intact; that part has, however, been given an add-on of minor yet fundamental change.

And so for the elderly Belgian couples who come to have coffee there as they have done for the past many years, the Indian bartender plays the role fulfilled by several earlier generations of native Antwerpian bartenders towards such clientele: producing small talk and a bit of neighborhood gossip, serving them their cups of coffee with a slightly overdone grace and friendliness, advising them on which cake to choose and so forth. The new owners behave towards their elderly regulars in a way as if they had run the place for decades. For the younger couples in the neighborhood, that same bartender is the head of an exotic food place, someone who answers questions about the origins and the ingredients of the biryanis they intend to savor, and someone who coaches them in the correct ways of having a 'real' Indian meal.

In Bellefleur, several of the developments we described in earlier chapters converge. Three different groups of the population enter into a polycentric space and cooperate there in different kinds of joint activities: the retired native working class people who have lived in the neighborhood for many decades; the younger and recently immigrated Belgian middle-class people; and members of the complex and volatile recent immigration into the neighborhood. The dominant image of the tavern is one of continuity: everything looks the same as before, and the food one could get there years ago can still be obtained now – and it is still quite nice. Within that continuity, however, a fundamental change has taken place: Bellefleur is now owned by newly immigrated people from India, and they now add an 'Indian accent' to the continuity in the menu.

This transition produces a complex and polycentric place, where highly diverse audiences can be addressed by people whose roles and identities change according to the audience and the activity in front of them. Different histories converge in simple routine activities, such as ordering a cup of coffee, and the complex socio-demographic make-up of the neighborhood can be distilled from observing who are having coffee and cake and who are having biryani dishes – and who serves both. And all of this can be spotted in the curious combinations we read on their menu – a public sign, as usual a detail. It is quite extraordinary and very rare indeed to find beef stew in trappist beer next to mutton kottu rotty on one menu in Antwerp. The changed menu was the very first indication for me that the place had changed; I could confirm it when I entered Bellefleur with some members of our research team and had lunch there: a delicious choice of Indian dishes with beers and soft drinks for seven people, all of that for 65 Euro.

Let us keep this example in mind when we engage now with a series of reflections.

The Order of Superdiversity

There is a long tradition of describing places such as Bellefleur as 'hybrid', 'multicultural', 'syncretic', 'cosmopolitan' and so on. They would be instances of 'vernacular globalization' in the sense of Appadurai (1996): the colorful blends of locality and globality that emblematically characterize contemporary cosmopolitan societies (see for instance, Mankekar, 2002; Wilson, 2006). I would argue that through examples such as this one, we begin to see the order of superdiversity.

This order, I said above, is best defined as complexity. This is evident, I believe, from the demonstrations given in the different chapters here and from the example of Bellefleur above. We have seen a multitude of crisscrossing and overlapping features of diversity, packed within a relatively small area and causing there something that could, even in a loosely descriptive way, be called 'superdiversity'. But let me elaborate a bit on this theme.

When we speak of order in a complex system, this order is multiscalar, and different scales may display different kinds of order. Patterns that are conflictual at an interpersonal scale can contribute to cohesion at a higher scale, for instance, and I have described the exploitative labor relations between new business elites and the flexible workforce of new immigrants as cohesive in that sense: as cohesive at the scale of the neighborhood. Below that scale level, exploitation is inevitably fraught with conflicts, and one can witness heated and rather unfriendly discussions about wages and other labor conditions on street corners between possible employers and people seeking work. In a more general sense, I have used conviviality as a term to describe the general live-and-let-live attitude that characterizes life in the neighborhood at the highest scale-level: the general pattern of relationships in the area is friendly and cooperative. Naturally this does not, and should not, obscure various forms of conflict occurring at other scale levels. The neighborhood is characterized by deep socio-economic inequalities, and they are articulated in a wide variety of situations and patterns of activity; conviviality is the broad shell within which several non-convivial processes can take place.

The same applies to power. There is not one single regime of power in my neighborhood, and no single group can be said to be in power everywhere and all of the time. There are times when shopkeepers and shoppers dominate the neighborhood, but of course, these times are never at night when shops are closed. The neighborhood is then dominated by several groups, some of which are rarely seen during the day. Power and control are dispersed over different groups, located in different sites and operating with different scopes and degrees of impact. Power, like the neighborhood, is complex and multiscalar.

Second, such order is dynamic, it is the opposite of the stability usually associated with the term order. Things change, and change is the system. Thus we get what Prigogine and Stengers (1984: 206) called 'unstable but not arbitrary' systems, systems that are perpetually in motion, and perpetually in the complex layered ways I just discussed, with motion – within-motion–within-motion. At the same time, the general (not the precise) vector of change can be determined: we can distinguish broader patterns in the seemingly chaotic processes of change, and we can, thus, generalize on the basis of these patterns, though we can only do that under specific conditions and in particular ways. I will return to this topic below, when I address the notion of structure.

When change is the system, this means that no single 'snapshot' will be 'representative'; take a snapshot the next day and the object will be different, because it has changed. Thus, by the time this book reaches the shelves of its readers, the neighborhood described here will have changed again, and many of the illustrations used in this book will not be found anymore. Several illustrations I used in this book were, in fact, pictures of closed shops. At least one of them has been recently reopened as a cheap textile store. The experiment cannot be repeated, thus, and the reason for that is straightforward: we did not perform an experiment, but described and analyzed a dynamic system continuously in motion. We were observing something the parameters of which were not within our control, we could not create a single situation to test the validity of hypotheses – a real social environment does not easily tolerate such interferences.

This has, remarkably, quite severe methodological consequences. In ethnography and in most other social sciences and humanities, we tend to work on the basis of a bounded set of evidence – a sample of data, a corpus of texts, a finite collection of artifacts reflecting fieldwork and having a specific moment of beginning and one of ending. We also have this idea of boundedness inscribed into the micro-objects we investigate: a conversation is said to have an 'opening' and a 'closing'; the same goes for a narrative, and in sociolinguistics, a term such as 'event' has for decades carried the suggestion of boundedness and definability – it was something that was self-contained and could thus be autonomously investigated.

Now, when we see change as the most central defining feature of our object, we must surrender the idea of boundedness. There is no beginning and no end to the patterns I described in the previous chapters; and as said above, no single moment of observation can capture the system in stasis, in equilibrium. We always and only observe moments in long sequences of change – a particular moment in a history that cannot be stopped by us, even if we would love it to stop as soon as we finish our analysis. The way it was then is the way it still is and will forever be – this classic structuralist assumption has no purchase anymore.

I can easiest illustrate this by referring to my own experiences with working on this book. The plan for it emerged many years ago, certainly as early as 2003 when my first sets of notes in view of this book were written. The plan was based on my life in the neighborhood, my 'deep hanging out', so to speak (Juffermans, 2010), which increasingly became dominated by a fascination for the bewildering diversity of people and languages I noticed around me. So I started this book many years ago, but was never able to complete it because I never had the impression that I had a complete, comprehensive and definitive image of my neighborhood. My 'informants', to use a weathered anthropological term, were unpleasant enough to change location perpetually, to casually open shops and close, rename or relocate them, to pass them on to people of an entirely different group – in short, my informants simply *wouldn't sit still* so that I could comfortably describe them 'the way they were'.

I was only able to complete this book when I began to understand that this was precisely the point: there *is* no position that can yield such a comprehensive and definitive picture, no position from where we can *completely* know whatever there is to be known.

What we do know, however, is this. The moment-in-history we observe points backwards to its past, sideways to its syntagmatic position and forward to its future; we can see this from observing the present as a deeply contextualized given. We can detect the historicity of the present condition, and from an analysis of the present we can make judgments about the probability of future developments. I will elaborate this further in the section on structure. So surrendering the ideal of comprehensive and definitive knowledge of a system comes with a bonus: we can now know and understand the dynamics of the system, its movements and metamorphoses.

This has a whole range of practical effects on research, and an attempt to review all of them would soon carry me into another book project. For now, let me say that we will be forced to reconsider quite radically what we mean by 'data', by 'evidence' – by *what* it is, *what* specifically, that data effectively demonstrate. Practices such as fieldwork will necessarily have to be drawn into these considerations, because in view of what I said just now, the necessary boundedness of fieldwork in practice makes representativity highly problematic, and thus raises the question: when do you have 'enough' data to describe a system? And which particular data will effectively be adequate for describing it? Below, when I discuss the prospects for interdisciplinarity, some tentative answers to these questions can be given. But one can already anticipate that comparative work acquires new complications, and that longitudinal study may hold specific advantages. A lot of what I could bring in this book could only be formulated because of my longitudinal exposure and presence in this neighborhood. One can naturally only observe change when one stays around long enough to notice it, and slow ethnographic monitoring quickly replaces hit-and-run ethnography as a useful method (cf. Van der Aa & Blommaert, 2011).

Now that we begin to get a glimpse of what the order of superdiversity consists of, our theoretical, conceptual and methodological toolkit must be adjusted so as to capture what we believe we need to capture: the logic of change instead of the 'laws' of the system, the deep immutable, timeless and static features that make the system into what it is, its generative grammar so to speak. We have to look for structures, indeed – the same targets remain in place – but structure understood in an entirely different sense now. Let me turn to that topic.

On Structure

What exactly do we mean when we mention the term 'structure'? Usually, we refer to a form of stability, a recurrent characteristic that defines not single cases but sets and categories of cases. A structure is a generalization – regularities across cases are defined by it – and a projection of an image of a chunk of reality, as the stable, static and timeless characteristics of a system that otherwise can be highly changeable. This is the structure of classical structuralism.

In actual fact, and empirically, something to which we give the label of 'structure' is often a feature that is subject to *slow change*. Empirically, we see a structure when we encounter enduring features, features that only change at a very slow pace – structure is the *durée* in a system. Slow change, of course, is change nonetheless, and a structure can therefore never be a *stable* feature, a feature that *does not change*. It is a feature that changes at a slower pace than others. And – this is crucial – a structure operates along all sorts of features that have a shorter lifespan and a higher pace of change and development. So if we look for structures, we cannot do that *against* or *in contrast to* fast-changing aspects of the system. The stochastic character of the system compels us to see structures in interaction with other features, and we keep in mind that all sorts of non-structural, exceptional and deviant features can cause massive changes in the system – can recreate structures, we can say. Prigogine and Stengers (1984: 178) emphasize this strongly. What they call 'fluctuations' – small deviations, statistically insignificant at first sight – can actually create an entirely new order, re-structuring, literally, the whole system: the famous butterfly effect. If we now recall the Bellefleur example, we see how a minor intervention – adding some Indian dishes to the Ur-Belgian menu – reshaped the place into an entirely different infra-structure, from a place mainly catering for elderly Belgians to one also cater-ing for the younger and more cosmopolitan inhabitants, and as an Indian-owned business networked with other Indian-owned businesses in the neighborhood and employing new immigrants in the kitchen.

We encountered an example of more enduring features when we discussed the ecumenical Dutch of the younger and upwardly mobile Turkish-origin entrepreneurs in the neighborhood. I noted, then, that we could see how an old order persisted while a new one came into place. While financially these new entrepreneurs firmly belong to the elite of the neighborhood, another feature – their accented Dutch – kept them back into the broad strata of immi-grants in the neighborhood (and beyond). Immigrant accent in Dutch is, thus, a structure, a feature of the system that appears to change very slowly, slower in any event than the financial and social position of its speakers.

It is the presence of such enduring features that enables us to make generalizations (the structures we identify do indeed bring a large set of individual cases together), and also affords us a degree of predictability in a system that otherwise looks entirely unpredictable. Again, however, our predictions are of a particular kind, for they are bounded by the limits of the life-cycle of the feature on which they are based. We can, therefore, only make predictions *over a specific span of time*. An example will clarify that.

Remember the remarks I made in Chapter 5 about the renovation of the Statiestraat–Driekoningenstraat. The City Council's ambition was to restore the street back to its original glory: as a flourishing shopping street with plenty of 'better' shops replacing the current landscape of night shops, ethnic groceries and internet shops. I explained that this ambition was not realized: the area did not become gentrified in the way anticipated by the authorities. I also pointed towards entirely different signs of gentrification: the immigration of younger, highly qualified double-income Belgians in the neighborhood, and the upward mobility of younger Turkish-origin entrepreneurs.

The failure of the City Council's plan for the gentrification of the area was to some extent predictable, and we must look at nonlinear processes in order to understand that. 'Better' shops demand different customers: high-income and quality-seeking customers. In my neighborhood, such customers could possibly be found among the community of newly immigrated Belgian double-income couples. There is, however, one problem: the actual time organization of the lives of double-income couples which, as a rule, involves leaving home before 8am for work and returning after 6pm – after the closing time of most shops, in other words. Thus – here is a nonlinear effect – the Belgian middle-class people are better served by ethnic groceries and night shops; the former usually remain open until 8pm; the latter can be open all night long. An infrastructure typically seen as an infrastructure of poverty appears to be an infrastructure for middle-class people as well. These people would also be best served by cheap late-night or take-away restaurants, and they appear to enjoy the Indian food at Bellefleur – in fact, many of the infrastructures of superdiversity work well for them.

This relatively uniform pattern of time organization among this category of people makes a number of things relatively predictable. For instance, it is relatively predictable that a regular supermarket with regular opening hours – from 9am to 6pm – would not attract too much business from among its target audience; the same goes for, say, a boutique selling top-of-the-range clothes, keeping the same opening hours. The supermarket and the boutique could do well, perhaps, on Saturday; but business would probably be quite slow during the working week. This is as relatively predictable as other rather widespread features of that category of people: the fact that they prefer brand products, that they buy and read books, and prefer Apple computers and phones over others, for instance.

As long as the structural organization of labor for this category of people remains stable, the patterns of behavior of members of that group will be 'structural' and subject to only very slow processes of change. We have found here a 'law of today', an enduring pattern that makes certain things relatively predictable and generalizable.

But I stressed that these predictions are confined to the life-cycle of the feature they describe. I just explained that the present infrastructures in the neighborhood are most adequate for 'non-typical' audiences, such as the Belgian middle-class. Many members of this group migrated into the neighborhood in their thirties or early forties. That means that, if the infrastructures in the neighborhood would stay the same, the people now well served by them would probably find them inadequate about thirty years from now, when the present cohort of relatively young and mobile people would be retired or close to retirement. Their lifestyle would profoundly change then – they would be able to do shopping, for instance, all day every day – and the infrastructures in the neighborhood will no longer be adequate for them. We can, then, anticipate conflicts emerging from the clash between supply and demand in the neighborhood, as well as, surely, emigration of elderly middle-class Belgians to other areas. As for Bellefleur, if it still exists by then, our cohort will probably be ordering coffee and cake rather than chicken biryani.

This is what Prigogine and Stengers called 'unstable but not arbitrary' systems. Through the mass of separate processes in this polycentric and multiscalar system, we can distinguish relatively enduring features that have a more extended life-span and that are not subject to the rapid change that characterizes other features, and are not restricted to isolated cases but characterize and tie together categories of cases. They offer us a level of systemic and structural description and interpretation, and they enable us to make generalizations.

The End of Synchrony

The two sets of reflections above – on the order of superdiversity and on structure – lead to an inevitable conclusion: the end of the 'Saussurean' synchrony in our fields of study. I already addressed part of this issue in Chapter 2; let me return to the point and elaborate it. I will bring two separate arguments to this claim: one about ethnography, the other about complexity.

(1) Ethnography always historicizes; both as a method and as an epistemology, it is an intrinsically historical enterprise. This is perhaps counterintuitive given the 'snapshot' impression often given by ethnographic description. Yet it is compelling because, if we wish to understand the synchronic array of features that compose any sign deployed in human activity, we need to disentangle the many pathways through which these features entered the synchronic sign. We can only understand signs, in other words, by reading back into their genesis and their trajectories of becoming. This, I argued in Chapters 2 and 3, is the analysis of signs as invested by histories of use and judgment – the very stuff, then, that makes them synchronically and syntagmatically meaningful.

As I have emphasized in several places here, signs only become meaningful and deployable *as* signs because they have been moved in place, so to speak, as possible resources for specific communicative tasks. These processes are 'pre-textual' (Blommaert, 2005b: 77) and systemic: they long precede the synchronic deployment of signs, and they determine not single instances of use, but categories of use. Their 'contextual' deployment only makes sense to the extent that context can be understood in relation to pre-texts – that we can establish a connection between what is being said now and what has been said before; between the present meaning of words and the meaning they had before and elsewhere. The notion of contextualization cues developed by Gumperz (1982) precisely stands for such connections between synchronic deployment and intertextual, indexical meaning resources.

In an ethnographic project, therefore, *simply nothing is really synchronic*. Whatever is meaningful is recognizable 'as something', and thus connected to long or short histories of use and evaluation. Ethnography and synchrony do not work together well.

(2) A complexity perspective, likewise, makes a synchronic position entirely impossible because, here too, we can only understand the present in terms of its arrow of time – its past and its future. Synchronic occurrence, we know, is 'synchronized' occurrence: a configuration of highly divergent histories collapsing in one moment of meaning making. The only object we can observe in real life are these synchronized occurrences – hence the power of synchrony as a frame for thinking about such objects. But we can only understand these occurrences by dissecting the different, complex and highly dynamic features of which they consist.

The reflections on structure made above historicize (and so destroy) the very core of synchrony as a paradigm. Structures, as I argued, were imagined as timeless and stable; it was the prominence of such structures as the real target of structuralist analysis that generated the Saussurean synchrony: we could observe the present and extract from it the absolute, timeless and stable 'laws'. These laws, then, made reoccurrences entirely predictable and so made contextualized inquiry redundant. No matter how much contextual 'noise' or 'fluctuation', the structures would always be there. It is when we begin to see such structures for what they really are – enduring features that have a long life cycle and change very slowly – that we begin to lay the foundations for a science of real social life. This science will, alas, lack the comfort of stability, absolute predictability and harmony of explanation that characterized the previous one. It will be a science of complexity in which we will forever be forced to look into the many different threads that generated the moment of occurrence that we observed.

On Interdisciplinarity

The latter point naturally brings me to the interaction between the kind of sociolinguistics I have advocated here, and related developments and concerns in adjacent sciences. The question is: what can this type of sociolinguistics offer to other disciplines? And I believe the answer lies in what I argued in the previous section.

The ethnographic perspective on LLS I outlined here combines two things: a strongly developed disciplinary concern with momentary, uniquely situated cases *and* a methodology that compels us to historicize these unique cases, to understand them as an interplay – a *complex* interplay – of systemic and non-systemic features co-occurring within one sign. This is the 'nano-sociolinguistics' that Parkin (2013) described: a discipline that digs into the smallest details of momentary events, but propels them towards the highest levels of contextual determination. We operate on *layered* objects in which a lot is 'unstable but not arbitrary'.

This particular ethnographic mode enables us to catch features of a system that very few other disciplines are prepared for: the very quick, almost immediate moments of change, the 'fluctuations' that escape the eye of scholars interested in structural and systemic features of the system. We can capture the dynamics of change years before it shows up in statistics, and very often entirely at odds with what policy papers and development plans assume. And if we apply the historicization I have consistently advocated here, our analyses of momentary change are not enclosed or isolated: we can set them into the broader framework of 'deep' change within a system, and so add a vital level of description and interpretation to more broadly and generally formulated modes of research (cf Blommaert & Rampton, 2011).

I have no doubt that this contribution would be welcomed by researchers from other disciplines. Scanning a broad literature in several fields, it is not hard to see the sharedness of concerns and interests. Polycentricity and complexity, for instance, have been used widely in urban studies and social geography (e.g. Buzar et al., 2007; Shearmur et al., 2007); scales and multiscalar phenomena have occupied people in the same disciplines (e.g. Swyngedouw, 1996; Uitermark, 2002); the broader transitions from multicultural to superdiverse societies have been extensively documented by Vertovec (2006, 2007, 2010). There is extensive common ground, and sociolinguistics has something unique to contribute to efforts to grasp the changed nature of our contemporary societies.

The uniqueness in our contribution lies in the way in which we read linguistic landscapes. They are not just indicators of a particular demographic composition, and they are even less interesting as rather evident pointers towards (stable) societal multilingualism. In our approach, superdiverse linguistic landscapes become historical documents, layered-simultaneous outcomes of different histories of people, communities and activities in ever-changing compositions – they become uniquely informative chronicles of complexity.

References

Agha, A. (2007) *Language and Social Structure*. Cambridge: Cambridge University Press.

Ardener, E. (1971) Social anthropology and the historicity of historical linguistics. In E. Ardener (ed.) *Social Anthropology and Language* (pp. 209–242). London: Tavistock.

Appadurai, A. (1996) *Modernity at Large*. Minneapolis: University of Minnesota Press.

Backhaus, P. (2007) *Linguistic Landscapes: A Comparative Study of Urban Multilingualism in Tokyo*. Clevedon: Multilingual Matters.

Backus, A. (2012) A usage-based approach to borrowability. *Tilburg Papers in Culture Studies*, paper 27.

Barni, M. (2008) Mapping immigrant languages in Italy. In M. Barni and G. Extra (eds) *Mapping Linguistic Diversity in Multicultural Contexts* (pp. 217–244). Berlin: Mouton de Gruyter.

Barni, M. and Bagna, C. (2008) A mapping technique and the linguistic landscape. In E. Shohamy and D. Gorter (eds) *Linguistic Landscape: Expanding the Scenery* (pp. 126–140). London: Routledge.

Barni, M. and Extra, G. (eds) (2008) *Mapping Linguistic Diversity in Multicultural Contexts*. Berlin: Mouton de Gruyter.

Bauman, R. and Briggs, C. (1990) Poetics and performance as critical perspectives on language and social life. *Annual Review of Anthropology* 19, 59–88.

Ben-Rafael, E., Shohamy, E., Amara, M.H. and Trumper-Hecht, N. (2006) Linguistic landscape as symbolic construction of the public space: The case of Israel. *International Journal of Multilingualism* 3, 7–30.

Beyens, K., Blommaert, J., Dewilde, A., Hillewaert, S., Meert, H., Stuyck, K. and Verfaille, K. (2005) *Grenzen aan de Solidariteit*. Gent: Academia Press.

Blackledge, A. and Creese, A. (2010) *Multilingualism: A Critical Perspective*. London: Continuum.

Blommaert, J. (2005a) Bourdieu the ethnographer: The ethnographic grounding of *habitus* and voice. *The Translator* 11/2: 219–236.

Blommaert, J. (2005b) *Discourse: A Critical Introduction*. Cambridge: Cambridge University Press.

Blommaert, J. (2008) *Grassroots Literacy: Writing, Identity and Voice in Central Africa*. London: Routledge.

Blommaert, J. (2010) *The Sociolinguistics of Globalization*. Cambridge: Cambridge University Press.

Blommaert, J. and Backus, A. (2012) Superdiverse repertoires and the individual. *Tilburg Papers in Culture Studies*, paper 24.

Blommaert, J., Collins, J. and Slembrouck, S. (2005) Spaces of multilingualism. *Language and Communication* 25, 197–216.

Blommaert, J. and Dong, J. (2010) *Ethnographic Fieldwork: A Beginner's Guide*. Bristol: Multilingual Matters.

Blommaert, J. and Huang, A. (2010) Historical bodies and historical space. *International Journal of Applied Linguistics* 6 (3), 267–282.

Blommaert, J. and Huang, A. (2010) Semiotic and spatial scope: Towards a materialist semiotics. *Working Papers in Urban Languages and Linguistics* 62. London, Gent, Albany and Tilburg.

Blommaert, J. and Rampton, B. (2011) Language and superdiversity. *Diversities* 13 (2), 1–22.

Blommaert, J. and Varis, P. (2012) Culture as accent. *Tilburg Papers in Culture Studies* 18.

Blommaert, J. and Verschueren, J. (1998) *Debating Diversity: Analysing the Discourse of Tolerance*. London: Routledge.

Bourdieu, P. (2004) Algerian landing. *Ethnography* 5 (4), 415–443.

Bourdieu, P. (1990) *The Logic of Practice*. Cambridge: Polity.

Buzar, S., Ogden, P., Hall, R., Haase, A., Kabisch, S. and Steinführer, A. (2007) Splintering urban populations: Emergent landscapes of reurbanisation in four European cities. *Urban Studies* 44 (4), 651–677.

Castells, M. (1996) *The Rise of the Network Society*. London: Blackwell.

Coupland, N. and Garrett, P. (2010) Linguistic landscapes, discursive frames and metacultural performance: The case of Welsh Patagonia. *International Journal of the Sociology of Language* 205, 7–36.

Creese, A. and Blackledge, A. (2010) Towards a sociolinguistics of superdiversity. *Zeitschrift für Erziehungswissenschaften* 13, 549–572.

Davidson, C. and Goldberg, D.T. (2010) *The Future of Thinking: Learning Institutions in a Digital Age*. Cambridge MA: MIT Press and MacArthur Foundation.

Eastman, C. and Stein, R.F. (1993) Language display. *Journal of Multilingual and Multicultural Development* 14, 187–202.

Eco, U. (1979) *A Theory of Semiotics*. Bloomington: Indiana University Press.

Fairclough, N. (1992) *Discourse and Social Change*. Cambridge: Polity Press.

Fabian, J. (1983) *Time and the Other: How Anthropology Makes its Object*. New York: Columbia University Press.

Fabian, J. (2001) *Anthropology with an Attitude*. Stanford: Stanford University Press.

Fabian, J. (2008) *Ethnography as Commentary*. Durham: Duke University Press.

Fishman, J. (1972) *The Sociology of Language: An Interdisciplinary Social Science Approach to Language in Society*. Rowley: Newbury House.

Fishman, J. and Garcia, O. (eds) (2010) *Handbook of Language and Ethnic Identity*. Oxford: Oxford University Press.

Foucault, M. (2001) (1977) 'L'oeil du pouvoir'. In *Dits et Ecrits II* (pp. 190–207). Paris: Gallimard.

Gieser, T. (2008) Embodiment, emotion and empathy: A phenomenological approach to apprenticeship learning. *Anthropological Theory* 8, 299–318.

Gorter, D. (2006) Introduction: The study of the linguistic landscape as a new approach to multilingualism. In D. Gorter (ed.) *Linguistic Landscape: A New Approach to Multilingualism* (pp. 1–6). Clevedon: Multilingual Matters.

Greimas, A.J. (1990) *Narrative Semiotics and Cognitive Discourses*. London: Pinter.

Gumperz, J. (1982) *Discourse Strategies*. Cambridge: Cambridge University Press.

Gumperz, J. and Hymes, D. (eds) (1972) *Directions in Sociolinguistics: The Ethnography of Communication*. New York: Holt, Rinehart and Winston.

Huang, A. (2010) London Chinatown: A sociolinguistic ethnography of visuality. PhD dissertation, University of Jyväskylä.

Hymes, D. (1972) Models of the interaction of language and social life. In J.J. Gumperz and D.H. Hymes (eds) *Directions in Sociolinguistics: The Ethnography of Communication* (pp. 35–71). London: Basil Blackwell (1986 edition).

Hymes, D. (1980) *Language in Education: Ethnolinguistic Essays*. Washington DC: Center for Applied Linguistics.

Hymes, D. (1996) *Ethnography, Linguistic, Narrative Inequality: Toward an Understanding of Voice*. London: Taylor & Francis.

Ingold, T. (2000) *The Perception of the Environment: Essays on Livelihood, Dwelling and Skill*. London: Routledge.

Irvine, J. and Gal, S. (2000) Language ideology and linguistic differentiation. In P. Kroskrity (ed.) *Regimes of Language* (pp. 35–83). Santa Fe: SAR Press.

Jackson, M. (1989) *Paths Toward a Clearing: Radical Empiricism and Ethnographic Inquiry*. Bloomington: Indiana University Press.

Jaworski, A. (2010) Linguistic landscapes on postcards: Tourist mediation and the sociolinguistic communities of contact. *Sociolinguistic Studies* 4 (3), 469–594.

Jaworski, A. and Thurlow, C. (2010) Language and the globalizing habitus of tourism: Towards a sociolinguistics of fleeting relationships. In N. Coupland (ed.) *Handbook of Language and Globalisation* (pp. 255–286). Oxford: Wiley-Blackwell.

Johnstone, B. (2008) *Discourse Analysis* (2nd edn). London: Blackwell.

Jørgensen, J-N., Karrebaek, M., Madsen, L. and Møller, J. (2011) Polylanguaging in super-diversity. *Diversities* 13 (2), 23–37.

Juffermans, K. (2010) Local languaging: Literacy products and practices in Gambian society. PhD Dissertation, Tilburg University.

Kress, G. (2009) *Multimodality: A Social Semiotic Approach to Contemporary Communication*. London and NY: Routledge.

Kress, G. and van Leeuwen, T. (1996) *Reading Images: The Grammar of Virtual Design*. London: Routledge.

Labov, W. (1963) The social motivation of a sound change. *Word* 19, 273–309.

Landry, R. and Bourhis, R.Y. (1997) Linguistic landscape and ethnographic vitality: An empirical study. *Journal of Language and Social Psychology* 16, 23–49.

Larsen-Freeman, D. (1997) Chaos/complexity science and second language acquisition. *Applied Linguistics* 18 (2), 141–165.

Lash, S. and Urry, J. (1994) *Economies of Signs and Space*. London: Sage.

Lefebvre, H. (2000) (1991) *The Production of Space*. Oxford: Blackwell.

Lin, P. (2009) Dissecting multilingual Beijng: The space and scale of vernacular globalization. *Visual Communication* 9 (1), 67–90.

Mankekar, P. (2002) 'India shopping': Indian grocery stores and transnational configurations of belonging. *Ethnos* 67 (1), 75–98.

Makoni, S. and Pennycook, A. (2007) *Disinventing and Reconstituting Languages*. Clevedon: Multilingual Matters.

Marshall-Fratani, R. (1998) Mediating the global and the local in Nigerian Pentecostalism. *Journal of Religion in Africa* 28 (3), 278–315.

Maskens, M. (2008) Migration et Pentecôtisme à Bruxelles. *Archives de Sciences Sociales des Religions* 143, 49–68.

Meeuwis, M. and Brisard, F. (1993) *Time and the Diagnosis of Language Change*. Antwerp: University of Antwerp (Antwerp Papers in Linguistics 72).

Meyer, B. (2006) *Religious Sensations: Why Media, Aesthetics, and Power Matter in the Study of Contemporary Religion*. Inaugural Lecture, Free University of Amsterdam.

Møller, J.S. and Jørgensen, J.N. (eds) (2011) *Language Enregisterment and Attitudes*. Copenhagen: Copenhagen Studies in Bilingualism.

Pachler, N., Makoe, P., Burns, M. and Blommaert, J. (2008) The things (we think) we (ought to) do: Ideological processes and practices in teaching. *Teaching and Teacher Education* 24, 437–450.

Parkin, D. (2013) Concluding comments. In J. Blommaert, B. Rampton and M. Spotti (eds) *Language and Superdiversity, Part 2*. *Special issue of Diversities* 14 (2), 71–83.

Pennycook, A. (2010) *Language as a Local Practice*. London: Routledge.

Pennycook, A. (2012) *Language and Mobility: Unexpected Places*. Bristol: Multilingual Matters.

Prigogine, I. and Stengers, I. (1984) *Order out of Chaos: Man's New Dialogue with Nature*. New York: Bantam Books.

Pype, K. (2009) 'We need to open up the country': Development and the Christian key scenario in the social space of Kinshasa's teleserials. *Journal of African Media Studies* 1 (1), 101–116.

Rampton, B. (1998) Speech Community. In J. Verschueren, J-O. Östman, J. Blommaert and C. Bulcaen (eds) *Handbook of Pragmatics* (pp. 1–34). Amsterdam: John Benjamins.

Rampton, B. (2006) *Language in Late Modernity*. Cambridge: Cambridge University Press.

Rampton, B. (2011) A neo-Hymesian trajectory in applied linguistics. *Working Papers in Urban Language and Literacies*, paper 78.

Saussure, F.de (1960) *Cours de Linguistique Générale* (eds C. Bally and A. Sechehaye), 3rd edition. Paris: Payot.

Scollon, R. (2001) *Mediated Discourse Analysis: The Nexus of Practice*. London: Routledge.

Scollon, R. (2008) Discourse itineraries: Nine processes of resemiotization. In V. Bhatia, J. Flowerdew and R. Jones (eds) *Advances in Discourse Studies* (pp. 233–244). London: Routledge.

Scollon, R. and Wong Scollon, S. (2003) *Discourses in Place: Language in the Material World*. London: Routledge.

Scollon, R. and Wong Scollon, S. (2004) *Nexus Analysis: Discourse and the emerging Internet*. London: Routledge.

Scollon, R. and Wong Scollon, S. (2009) Breakthrough into action. *Text and Talk* 29 (3), 277–294.

Sharma, D. and Rampton, B. (2011) Lectal focusing in interaction: A new methodology for the study of superdiverse speech. *Working Papers in Urban Language and Literacies*, paper 79.

Shearmur, R., Coffey, W., Dubé, C. and Barbonne, R. (2007) Intrametropolitan employment structure: Polycentricity, scatteration, dispersion and chaos in Tornot, Montreal and Vancouver, 1996–2001. *Urban Studies* 44 (9), 1713–1738.

Shohamy, E. and Gorter, D. (eds) (2009) *Linguistic Landscape: Expanding the Scenery*. London: Routledge.

Silverstein, M. (1996) Monoglot 'standard' in America: Standardization and metaphors of linguistic hegemony. In D. Brenneis and R. Macaulay (eds) *The Matrix of Language* (pp. 284–306). Boulder CO: Westview Press.

Silverstein, M. (2003) Indexical order and the dialectics of sociolinguistic life. *Language and Communication* 23, 193–229.

Silverstein, M. (2005) Axes of – E vals: Token vs. Type Interdiscursivity. *Journal of Linguistic Anthropology* 15, 6–22.

Silverstein, M. (2006) Pragmatic indexing. In K. Brown (ed.) *Encyclopedia of Language and Linguistics* (2nd edn, vol. 6; pp. 14–17). Amsterdam: Elsevier.

Silverstein, M. (2009) Does the autonomy of linguistics rest on the autonomy of syntax? An alternative framing of our object of study. Plenary paper, XXXVI Finnish Linguistics Conference, Jyväskylä, May 2009 (ms).

Silverstein, M. and Urban, G. (eds) (1996) *Natural Histories of Discourse*. Chicago: University of Chicago Press.

Stroud, C. and Mpendukana, S. (2009) Towards a material ethnography of linguistic landscape: Multilingualism, mobility and space in a South-African township. *Journal of Sociolinguistics* 13 (3), 363–383.

Swyngedouw, E. (1996) Reconstructing citizenship, the re-scaling of the State and the new authoritarianism: Closing the Belgian mines. *Urban Studies* 33 (8), 1499–1521.

Uitermark, J. (2002) Re-sacling, 'scale fragmentation' and the regulation of antagonistic relationships. *Progress in Human Geography* 26 (6), 743–765.

Van der Aa, J. (2012) Ethnographic monitoring: Language, narrative and voice in a Carribean classroom. PhD dissertation, Tilburg University.

Van der Aa, J. and Blommaert, J. (2011) Ethnographic monitoring: Hymes' unfinished business in education. *Anthropology and Education Quarterly* 42 (4), 319–334.

Vertovec, S. (2006) The emergence of super-diversity in Britain. Centre on Migration, Policy and Society, Working paper 25 (Oxford University).

Vertovec, S. (2007) Super-diversity and its implications. *Ethnic and Racial Studies* 30 (6), 1024–1054.

Vertovec, S. (2010) Towards post-multiculturalism? Changing communities, contexts and conditions of diversity. *International Social Science Journal* 199, 83–95.

Waddington, C.H. (1977) *Tools for Thought*. St Albans: Paladin.

Wang, X. (2013) Authenticities and globalization in the margins: A study of Enshi, China. PhD Dissertation, Tilburg University.

Weber, J-J. and Horner, K. (2012) *Introducing Multilingualism: A Social Approach*. London: Routledge.

Williams, G. (1992) *Sociolinguistics: A Sociological Critique*. London: Longman.

Wilson, D. (2006) Fuzhou flower shops of East Broadway: 'heat and noise' and the fashioning of new traditions. *Journal of Ethnic and Migration Studies* 32 (2), 291–308.

Index